University on the Heights

University on the Heights

on the Heights

EDITED BY WESLEY FIRST

Doubleday & Company, Inc., Garden City, New York

To J.B., guide, goad, and friend

Contents

Introduction

One is apt to think of a great university somewhat in terms of absolutes: the university is a tradition, founded upon readily identifiable building blocks such as curricula (trivium and quadrivium), hierarchy (the professor is the aristocrat, the students are plebes), precise requirements (124 points at a minimum grade equal the baccalaureate), and purpose (to produce the educated man).

Well, this is true in large measure about every great university of the Western world. It is true of Columbia, the University on Morningside Heights. But how this neat and exact schema collapses when one turns to the Columbia man! Ten young men will have entered Columbia College, say, at different points in time, and upon examination of the best evidence—their autobiographical expressions and the careers they have followed—we find they turn out to be so varied, so richly varied, that they might be thought to have attended ten different colleges. One man will have followed the precise pattern suggested above, while a second will not only not have graduated, but will not have discharged very many of the obligations and requirements. Yet a third will have done his undergraduate work elsewhere than at Columbia, and taken one or more graduate degrees at Columbia. The possibilities are endless, the combinations numberless.

There is, in spite of the lack of pattern, such a thing as the Columbia Man even if, as Professor Caplow points out, he may not be as easily recognizable as is the Yale Man. It is a fascinating exercise to see him, the Columbia Man, emerge out of this collection of essays by thirty-three persons who share for the purpose of this volume only one characteristic: each went to the University on the Heights for some part of his life.

This collection cuts across years. Gold was discovered in the Klondike the year one of our essayists entered Columbia College; Victoria was Queen and Empress, William Dean Howells and Stephen Crane were writing good stories, and Walt Whitman and Henry James were living literature and living men. Columbia College was a small collection of indifferent-looking buildings at Forty-ninth Street and Madison Avenue in Manhattan. The year another of our men graduated, Eisenhower defeated Stevenson and it was the time of the Silent Generation.

Different styles of men and writing are collected in this volume too: the measured prose of the scientist Lederberg, the graceful prose of Barzun and Trilling, the rollicking prose of Gallico, the serious and searching prose of Merton.

Here are the essays, then, by authors who have something of interest to say to every generation, whether connected with Columbia University or not—the younger looking back to what had been, the older looking forward to what was to be. The essays also say something of the writers in terms of literary and intellectual values, rather than simply of them as Columbia University men.

May you enjoy them as much as I enjoyed assembling them!

Thanks are due many persons, all of Columbia: Grayson Kirk, President, for enthusiastic endorsement and wise suggestions; Morris W. Watkins, Executive Secretary of the Alumni Federation, for a host of helpful hints and for labors in the sometimes musty archives; George C. Keller, Director of College Relations, for good guidance; Sharon Oswald and Bonnie Edwards, for secretarial assistance far above and beyond the call.

New York City   WESLEY FIRST

University on the Heights

Nathaniel Peffer

⅍⅌⅌⅍

by Mark Van Doren

At the Faculty Club I did not always lunch with members
of my own department, though I enjoyed that too, and most
of my noonday meals were taken in fact with them. But there
were days when I wandered afield—perhaps with the lawyers,
of whom I remember Jerome Michael best because he talked
so perfectly, achieving a precision that anyone might envy; or
with the historians; or with the physicists and mathemati-
cians; or with the biologists. The Club was, and of course
still is, a meeting place where anything might happen, where

MARK VAN DOREN, *1920 Ph.D., 1960 L.H.D., is the man
most mentioned by others in this collection. His teaching
career began at Columbia in 1920 and continued to 1959.
He has been critic, editor, and poet, winning the Pulitzer
Prize for Poetry in 1940.*

anything at all might sooner or later be said. And one day
a very startling thing was said to me. No consequences followed from it, yet I have never been able to forget it, nor have
I wanted to.

It was said by Nathaniel Peffer, who was lunching alone
and agreed that I might join him. I had known him for a
number of years as an expert on Far Eastern affairs; I had
read his articles, in *The Nation* and elsewhere; and latterly
I had been aware of his great distinction as a professor of
international relations at Columbia. Also, I must add, I had
been attracted to him by something gruff, something decisive,
in his voice and manner. This day the subject of doctoral
dissertations was on his mind—perhaps he was suffering under
an unusual number of them at the moment, though I do not
remember that he complained of this—and suddenly he
growled, "You know, we have entirely the wrong view of the
Ph.D. It shouldn't be given for a contribution to knowledge.
No man can make a contribution to knowledge before he is
sixty. It's nonsense to expect it from a young man. I read
these dissertations and I don't learn anything from them
that I really need to know. They don't change me. They
don't educate me."

I understood him, for I had been entertaining something
like the same conviction. But I had a question.

"What then would you have them do?"

"Who?"

"The candidates. On what grounds would you finally judge
them? They would have to convince you, wouldn't they, that
they deserved the degree?"

"Of course. Naturally. But there are other ways of doing
that."

"For instance."

"Well, what do we want to be convinced of? Not that they *have* made a contribution to knowledge, but that they are likely to do so before they are sixty—oh, say fifty—oh, say forty. What we need to know now is how well they understand the whole subject to which they are going to devote their lives, assuming that we grant them the permission. What are the chances that someday they will write something that everybody will have to read?"

"Excellent! But again, what would you have them do?"

"Write a long essay on the central issue in their field. In my case that would be war and peace. I would have all candidates for the Ph.D. in international relations write on the same subject. War and peace."

"Year after year?"

"Yes."

"Wouldn't that grow tiresome?" I was thinking of the readers, the professors, but he was thinking of the students.

"No great subject is tiring. They would grow as they considered it, and as they mastered its literature. They would be grateful, I tell you. And they might even begin to be original. The same subject wouldn't produce the same essay from every student. They would all be different—I'd bet on that. But from whatever a student wrote we might come to some conclusion about his promise. The best ones would be worth watching."

That is all I remember of the conversation, except that I remarked upon the triviality of certain literary dissertations I had recently read. They were trivial, I said, because their subjects were. Fringe subjects, desperately chosen so as not to conflict with others already treated.

"Fringe!" he said. "That's it. We want the center—always the center. Tiresome, you said. Well, what we get now is so tiresome I could howl. Contributions! I'm sick of contributions."

A number of years passed before I saw him again in similar circumstances, and then it may have been at the same table.

"Do you remember," I asked him, "what you once said to me about doctoral dissertations?"

"Yes."

"Do you still think what you thought then?"

"Yes."

"Have you ever proposed that it be done?"

"Yep."

"Has it been done?"

"Nope."

And that was that, although in after years I dreamed— I still do so—of students who somehow had not been permitted to miss the great, the powerful, the central things which, if they only knew it, lay open to their view. How many such students have there ever been? How many are there now? If the tribe increases, men like Nathaniel Peffer are the cause.

A Recollection of
Raymond Weaver

༷༺᛭༻༷

by *Lionel Trilling*

In my undergraduate days, no student ever referred to him
except as Buck Weaver. He must have known this, but he gave
no license to the name, and once when a young instructor,
who had been a student in the College, presumed to call
him by it, the witless youth was shriveled by Weaver's terrible
stare and vanished, none knows where. It was a good name
for him because it was at once absurdly incongruous and
exactly appropriate. So far as it came out of American folk
culture and smacked of the frontier——there are two persons

LIONEL TRILLING, *1925 College, 1926 M.A., 1938 Ph.D.,
taught at Wisconsin and Hunter before returning to Columbia
to start through the ranks as instructor of English in 1931
and become George Edward Woodberry Professor of Literature and Criticism.*

called Buck in *Huckleberry Finn* and Mark Twain notes the name as characteristic of the Southwest: "They called each other Bill, and Buck, and Hank . . . and talked lazy and drawly, and used considerable many cuss-words."—it was wonderfully at odds with Weaver's patrician appearance and manner, which had an English and even an Anglican cast: when George Hibbitt once recorded his speech, Weaver listened to the playback of the studied resonance and exclaimed, "Moy Gohd, do I speak like thaht?—I sound like a *Bishoppp!*" Which was very close to the mark—there was that in his demeanor which could be thought hieratic and even episcopal, rather more in the Church of England than in the Roman way; to be sure, one could not imagine him wearing gaiters (plus-fours and Argyle stockings, then in fashion, were something else again), but any of the ceremonial garments would have seemed apt to his dignity, to his sense of occasion, and to what might be called his belief in the sacramental nature of life.

And then, of course, he was a buck in the old Regency sense of the word—to us who were undergraduates in his earlier days, an important part of Weaver's *charisma* was the elegance of his appearance, a dandyism in which we recognized a moral implication, an element of discipline. His dandyism began with the erectness of his carriage and the spring of his step, of which, I always supposed, he was conscious. He was perhaps not quite so imperially slim as Richard Cory, but there was no doubt that he glittered when he walked. To see him cross the Van Am quadrangle was to have the sense that one was witnessing some striking detail of a moment in history, or the representation of that moment on the stage. He had the almost avowed intention of being both historic and histrionic. It was exactly his purpose to be a presence, a figure, to propose himself as dramatic and fully significant. He was splendidly endowed to carry out the intention, what with the famous eyebrows that lent terror to the famous minatory stare, which he could maintain for what seemed an eternity, the large mouth to which, if it suited his pedagogic need, he could summon an expression of demonstrative brutality, so that in his later years, one inevitably thought of Roman emperors, although in his youth he brought to mind Renaissance princes as well as prelates, and the countenance that somehow seemed to have been buffed and burnished to make it gleam. He affected porkpie hats and for many years he wore a full-cut overcoat of lightest gray tweed, which, although it was not at all *outré,* was worn with such an air that it transcended its existence as merely an overcoat to become a cloak. One came to know of him that he was the kind of dandy who gave distinction to what he wore—actually he made a point of not spending much money on dress—rather than the other way around. One also came to know that, although vanity certainly played its part in his dandyism, in that intention of his to be a figure and a presence, there was something else at work, a piety toward life, the wish to suggest that *it* was dramatic and significant by being so himself, the desire to propose this possibility to others, pre-eminently to his students. His long and perhaps only half-ironic involvement with astrology was no doubt an expression of his belief in the cosmic importance of human existence.

Such fame as Weaver had beyond the Columbia campus derived from a very considerable achievement. It was he who began the revival of Herman Melville's reputation. When

Melville died in 1891, he was, despite his early success, a forgotten man. In 1921 Weaver published his *Herman Melville, Mariner and Mystic* and Melville began to be seen as one of the great geniuses of American literature. A huge body of Melville scholarship and criticism was soon brought into being and, as it developed, Weaver's part in the salvage operation came to be largely forgotten. This was partly because, as Melville bulked ever larger in the American pantheon, it began to seem as if he must always have been where he belonged. But no doubt it was also because certain qualities of Weaver's book exposed it to depreciatory judgment. Its style is rather excessive in its rhetoric, overwrought, seeking too strenuously to be eloquent, sacrificing precision to this end. It was a style that might have passed in the twenties, although even then it was suspect, but it became ever less acceptable. Weaver wanted—I think, desperately —to be a writer. But his one novel, *Black Valley,* a commemoration of the time he had spent as a teacher in Japan, was not a success, nor was it really good, and after its publication there supervened, as I seemed to gather, a great difficulty in getting words on paper, so that even short pieces proved a torture for him, and Weaver turned all his intellectual energies to teaching.

Teaching meant for him teaching in Columbia College, which in turn meant being in inveterate antagonism to the graduate division of the English Department. He held its corporate existence in supreme contempt, from which, however, he exempted a few individual members. The book on Melville had been written, I believe, as a dissertation for the doctorate, but Weaver never took the degree, either because, as one story went, having completed all the requirements, he refused to pay some small statutory fee, or because he would not submit his book to be examined by judges whose judgment he did not respect. He never went further with his Melville studies, although it was he who found and published the manuscript of *Billy Budd, Foretopman,* a discovery that might have made the scholarly fortune of another man. Indeed, as he turned more and more to Dante and the Italian Renaissance, he came to regard Melville, with some irony, as too much a romantic. The idea of research and "publication" seemed ever more Philistine to him, representing the contrary principle to the humanism that he felt he must, and did, represent. The graduate division of the day repaid his antagonism more or less in kind and his promotion in the department was scandalously slow, and all the slower because his fierce pride forbade him to claim what was not given to him as of right.

It would be impossible for me to recall Raymond Weaver in a personal way without referring to the fact that for a good many years he constituted himself my enemy. The word has an archaic ring which makes it seem almost absurd, but Weaver's system of feeling *was* archaic, by choice, and as he made a cult of friendship, so he made a cult of enmity, both very Renaissance in their intensity. His hostility to me began when I was an undergraduate, a member of his General Honors section. He disliked me, I think, because he took me to be "intellectual," which I was not, although most of my friends were. But I did perhaps have a degree of skepticism or irony toward his way of looking at things, a deficiency of response to his enthusiasm for certain grand qualities of style and feeling, and the contemptuous flare of his demonstrative nostrils was often directed toward my coolness. Nothing could have been better calculated to increase Weaver's dislike than the manner of my appointment to the College English Department as an instructor, for I was not chosen by the Hamilton Hall professors themselves but imposed on them by the decree of the chairman of the department, Ashley Thorndike, an action that Weaver took to be an affront to the autonomy of the College, as indeed it was. Then, to make matters still worse, as I have come to see, after my first two or three years as an instructor I fell into a depressed state of feeling which was not to be hidden, and this Weaver could not endure. He refused to address me; when we passed each other in the halls, he cut me dead. It was largely through his urging that the department decided to terminate my appointment. And just at this point our relationship began to change. For I did not take my dismissal quietly but angrily. Since I was not on speaking terms with Weaver, he was not among the senior members of the department whom I sought out one by one to denounce for the vast stupidity of their action, but he was told of these interviews, and now, as we passed each other, he nodded to me, distantly but unmistakably; I existed. For a long time the work on my doctoral dissertation had gone slowly and badly; my expression of anger miraculously cleared my mind of doubts and hesitations and I finished the book in a maniacal burst of energy; it was well received by my examining committee, and the matter of the dismissal yielded to the question of whether or not I should be promoted. Weaver asked to read the manuscript, and in his beautiful India-ink script, derived both from his early training as an engineer and from the Renaissance chancery hand, he wrote me a kind letter about it. From then on all was peaceable between us. A certain distance always remained, but I think that Weaver as much as I regarded this as a positive rather than a negative element of our friendship.

I have no doubt of what happened to change Weaver's feeling toward me. He set great store by anger, which seemed to him a means of self-definition, an active as against a passive state. What he could understand as passivity in another person made him uncomfortable, very likely because it aroused in him, as it does in many, an impulse to cruelty. My display of anger reassured him; I was not to be so easily hurt as he thought. And then I had further redeemed myself by having *made* something; I can scarcely suppose that Weaver was in sympathy with the subject of my book, but he would have seen that I had written about Matthew Arnold *con amore*, with commitment, as a personal act, and such doctrine as the book might contain would be secondary in his interest to my having imposed my will on recalcitrant material and given it a shape. Although I never heard him refer to it, Weaver would have known and approved Yeats' division of the later history of Western culture into two epochs, the earlier one being characterized by the "nonchalance of the hand," which, having been lost, was replaced by the "gentle sensitive mind" of the modern age. To the "hand" Weaver gave all his allegiance. It was for him, one might say, the metaphor for the mind at its best, as it was associated with the body and expressed itself in the things that it shaped— the "shaping power" that Coleridge saw as the defining characteristic of the imagination Weaver assigned to mind as a whole. His Renaissance feeling for the "hand" was by no means only metaphorical. His own right hand was of peculiar interest to him, and during departmental meetings it would from time to time go through a little drill of flexing, clenching, and stretching which Weaver would observe with a sort of stern fondness; perhaps this activity of his hand had the purpose of assuring him that the world was actual, there to be comprehended, *grasped;* or perhaps it was his way of readying it for the work he put it to, playing the piano, painting, refinishing old furniture; he was proud of his irremediably stained fingernails.

His manual doctrine once disrupted my family life. Weaver met my wife for the first time at a cocktail party and he ended a long conversation with her by saying, "You think too much and you like words more than you should. Have you ever painted? You should paint." She looked at him in astonishment and said she could not even draw. "Drawing has nothing to do with painting," he said impatiently. "You must paint. I shall send you the materials." Panic overcame her when, on her questioning me, I told her that he would do as he had said. One day there arrived an elaborate box of oil paints, a sheaf of brushes, a palette, turpentine, canvas boards of all sizes. My wife took one look at the gift, burst into tears, said fiercely, "I won't, I just won't. He has no right to impose his will like that!" and hustled the stuff into a closet. But one morning, "because after all it would be rude not to," she got it out to try it. She was lost. For six weeks she painted every day and nearly all the day, neglecting everything else, astonished at her ability to represent objects (in those years still thought to be one of the legitimate ends of painting). Eventually she gave it up, partly because it took so much time as to make any other activity impossible, partly because she began to develop standards of performance she knew she would never meet. But she still says that the six weeks made the most contented time she ever experienced and she held Weaver in awe for knowing that this would be so.

Weaver's own work with his hands served the purposes not only of pleasure but also of survival. I once paid him a visit in his home and he showed me some old chairs he had bought cheaply at auction and was scraping down to the wood. Partly with sincerity, partly to show my sense of the attractiveness of his enterprise, I said that I would like to engage in it too and asked about auction rooms. He shook his head in emphatic negation, addressed me by name with a solemn intensity that took me aback, and said, "No. I do these things because I must. Last night until four o'clock I scraped flecks of paint off my kitchen range with a razor blade." No one, I think, would have supposed that Raymond Weaver led an unperturbed inner life, but never till then had I imagined the virulence of the evil spirits by which he was beset, or the heroism with which he struggled to hold them off, the activity of the hand defending the citadel of the mind. A natural word for him had always been "superb" and never did it seem more just than at that moment when, with a superb simplicity, he for a moment put aside his characteristic reserve out of the need to have his pain recognized. Beyond recognition no one would have presumed to go: one could not possibly pity the man who, in any meeting one had with him, had the power of making life seem larger than life.

Early Columbia
Reminiscences

ᔰᔰ᛭᛭ᔰᔰ

by Hugh Auchincloss Brown

Columbia College became Columbia University in 1896 and
in 1897 moved from Forty-ninth Street and Madison Avenue
to Morningside Heights, so that my class of 1900 had only
one year at Forty-ninth Street. At that time we still had
horse cars and elevated railroads with cars pulled by little
dinkey steam engines that burned anthracite coal and did
not produce too much smoke. In those days saloons competed
by offering large and larger schooners of beer for five cents,
and whiskey at the bars was two for a quarter, with the

HUGH AUCHINCLOSS BROWN, *1900 E.E., president of the
Society of Forty Niners, did fifty years of research for his
book,* Cataclysms of the Earth, *which gives a plausible geo-
logical explanation of the flood of Noah's day, and proposes
the means of preventing a possible repetition.*

bartender handing you the bottle and allowing you to pour your own size drink. Many of us paid little attention to alcoholic beverages until the prohibition laws made us feel the need for social drinks.

One of our most highly respected and admired professors was Charles Frederick Chandler, who amazed me one day by saying that he had his doubts about gravitation being an attraction of mass for mass. Holy smoke, I thought, Chandler questions the "Attraction of Gravity"; maybe he might question Adam and Eve, which was then, to me, equally fundamental. I knew that I was expected to think as well as absorb knowledge, so two years later I raised my hand in a class conducted by Mr. Townsend and said, "You tell me that there is an attraction of gravity that increases directly as the mass and inversely as the square of the distance, yet you also tell me that falling bodies move at a constant acceleration of gravity of about thirty-two feet per second for each consecutive second of the fall. Which is correct?" Townsend's face flushed red while he said that he could assure me that both were correct. He evidently reported that to Professor Francis B. Crocker, who headed the School of Electrical Engineering, for Crocker, as my classmate John Kebler insisted, told him that I was a whiz; and that probably had something to do with my business career starting with Crocker-Wheeler Company of Ampere, New Jersey. Both were Columbia men and Gano Dunn, 1893, was the brilliant chief engineer.

Our distinguished Professor Michael I. Pupin, whose inventions made long-distance telephone conversations possible, rose highly in the esteem of our class when he offered to lick me and then offered to lick any man in the class. I had tried to terminate his lecture on thermodynamics by picking up my books, then put them back on the floor and again picked them up to show that the lecture was over. He said he would take me out and lick me if I did that again. Years later, on reading his excellent book *Immigrant to Inventor,* I realized that he was not bluffing.

John Erskine, a classmate proficient in literature and music, but best known for his book *The Private Life of Helen of Troy,* records the awe he felt on arriving from rural New Jersey, in horse and buggy, to become a Columbia freshman. His classmates seemed to him so mature and sure of themselves at first; but only temporarily.

At a very early alumni meeting with another classmate who became distinguished, Professor William King Gregory, I told him that his theory of evolution was "all wet." He merely laughed. Later, when I came to understand mutations, I told him how wrong I had been. Then we both laughed. When I got hold of a copy of his superb two-volume masterpiece, *Evolution Emerging,* I realized his eminence.

William Russell Grace of our class, son of a former mayor of New York City, used to drive to Columbia in a phaeton, get out about a block away and walk, while the coachman drove home. I recall that he had trouble with calculus; but he did not need an engineering degree to succeed in business. The last time I met him he was president of Ingersoll-Rand Corporation.

My recollection is that none of my classmates had any idea of future employment, except those planning to join their parents' interests; the only idea was to get a college education. But I learn that some faculty members think that students know just what they expect to become after graduation. In my own case I think that I was more interested in making the varsity baseball team than in getting a degree of E.E., but I knew that to stay on the team I must pass my examinations.

Of the men who attended classes at Forty-ninth Street there are now about sixty surviving veterans, all members of The Society of Forty Niners, sometimes called The Grand Army of Columbia. For about sixty years we held annual reunion dinner meetings, and Henry Krumb, 1898, generally picked up the tab for the deficiencies. He later showed his appreciation for Columbia by such an extremely large bequest that our venerable School of Mines is now named for Henry.

The Army That Never Ran Away

≫⁙⁙⁙≪

by David Cort

In my time at Columbia, the early twenties, we were totally a-political. If we had ever known that Whittaker Chambers and various other people were drifting toward communism, we would have thought they had gone to the Moon. A Czarist anthem was one of the sentimental waltz tunes of the period. Nobody had any intention of ever voting. The political operation was considered a sort of grimy joke.

Still, the faculty and administration considered a few of us, chiefly the editors of *Jester,* as virtual Bolsheviks. My dazzling predecessor on *Jester,* Corey Ford, wrote two para-

DAVID CORT, *1924 College and a* Jester *alumnus, has been a writer and editor from the beginning. His name has been attached to* Vanity Fair, Vogue, Time, Life, United Nations World, Nation, *and to books.*

graphs that fired a riot at the next Columbia-N.Y.U. football game. This is writing, I mean, writing.

The odd thing was that, amidst all the grandiose architecture, the truly beloved building was the down-at-heels brick nothing called East Hall, off the southeast corner of Low Library. The stairs creaked, the wooden floors sagged, there was a definite smell, *Jester* had one tiny room on the third floor with a lion's head, and for me it was Columbia.

I will never forget a geology professor named Galloway, whose class included Corey, myself, and Tom Wenning, later president of the New York Critics' Circle. Galloway put us on the honor system. One day somebody noticed that he had crept in and was peeking at us from behind the coats (this in Schermerhorn Hall). From that time on, we all agreed to cheat, all except Ford and Wenning, who studied together and, for some inscrutable reason, liked the course. Ford was expelled for cheating. The real reason was that he had parodied, *sotto voce*, Galloway's solecisms under his nose, and that Wenning could not suppress his laughter. But in fact Ford and Wenning were the only non-cheaters. Such a man leaves a memorable impression on boys. I can still see Galloway. His memory conditions my opinion of any possible academic community, and always will. Nor, in terms of Columbia, do I think it desirable for this Neanderthal to have insulted Corey Ford.

Columbia in that period was loaded with talent. Too many of those young men remained dumb in the outside world, for various reasons, or died too soon. I still remember with admiration and affection Pinky Jordan, Charlie Eliason, Bill Stahl, Gene Wright, John Slavik, Dick Fox, Don Freeman, Bob Hale, Bill Meloney. Others, who made a notable mark, were Corey Ford, Tom Wenning, Rondo Robinson, Lynd Ward, Allan Keller, Teddy Bernstein, Fadiman, Bessie, Endore, Dick Watts, Horace Coon, Freddy Packard, Jud Phillips, Warner Bellah, Ted Shane, not to speak of Whittaker Chambers.

I speak primarily for *Jester,* and I have never since been so delighted by my companions, or aspired to nobler company. In that brief golden age, *Jester* was an indubitable Olympus to its inhabitants, so awesome to outsiders that a present Columbia professor modestly told the writer, "With a bottle of gin in 504 Hartley, some very good things are said there too." I agreed that this was not impossible, and passed on. But I was shocked by his humility, which he has since shaken off.

Boys as grandees may offend some people. They do not offend me, for the current crop is too like the boys I knew. One can never forget, nor wish to forget, having been a member of a good company, and every member of such a company must be a grandee.

In a tradition as old as Columbia, I was, as an undergraduate, the sworn foe of the administration, specifically Hawkes, Fackenthal, Coss, Knox—and not particularly interested by any of the faculty. What amazed me was that grown men could be so easily outwitted and infuriated by a boy—I was then eighteen years old. I had no love for the sacred-cow course in Contemporary Civilization, which seemed to me to be telling me what to think about what I could better read in the newspaper. Hawkes once informed me that Columbia planned to mold my character; I replied that he could try to do what he liked with my brain but that my character was entirely in the hands of my parents and myself. Obviously no dialogue was possible. Hawkes did everything possible to prevent my graduation (details on request) and at my commencement, when I tried to introduce him to my mother, he turned brusquely on his heel. He was a very sincere man.

What really formed our characters in the early twenties was Columbia's losing football team. Once one has diagnosed a football defeat by Williams as a moral victory for Columbia, one can never again desert a cause merely because it seems to be losing. Columbia in those days could accept monotonous defeat. It was an army that never ran away.

None of these disillusionments turned us against Columbia. How could they? We felt we were Columbia. We simply did not believe that these other gentlemen, graduates usually of other colleges, stood for the tradition. We had either intuitively grasped, or invented, the tradition and we felt at home in it. Many men's almost mystical love for Columbia, and other men's indifference, may be explained by the fact that it is a difficult and arcane love, too difficult for some. Harvard, Yale, and Princeton are reasonably simple, coherent phenomena. Columbia is not and never will be. Hawkes, for example, had a simple vision of Columbia as a place where he could elevate underdogs. He was baffled when he met someone who did not feel like an underdog. This was unforgivable to Hawkes, the farm boy doing an imitation of rough-hewn granite. His famous battles came later with the proletarians, Reed Harris and James Wechsler, but his true rage was reserved for gentlemen.

The prohibition amendment was important for the early twenties, as an invitation to ruin for some. At first we bought Gordon's Gin at the nearest drugstore. In a year or so speakeasies appeared nearby dispensing needle beer. Still later we went to midtown and Greenwich Village speakeasies and a weird rendezvous called The Redhead where the owners of the famous "21" got their start (around the corner from the present offices of *The Nation*), an incredible seventeenth-century brawling place where all the girls were thought to have syphilis. *Jester* once challenged the drinking society, Kappa Beta Phi, to a beer-drinking contest. The *Jester* team eliminations, held on the third floor of East Hall with a keg of needle beer, were observed by a Kappa Beta Phi delegation. All the "observers" had dropped out at around fifteen steins, while ten *Jester* men remained. (There were watchmen at the toilet to see that nobody threw up.) I believe I got past thirty steins, but I was defeated by Pinky Jordan, who was even younger than I. We were both heroes and supported across the campus, virtually floating, to our fraternity houses. We tactfully dropped the idea of the contest. I still don't know how Pinky did it. We must both have had splendid metabolisms, but Pinky had the motivation, God bless his soul.

Lacking only $100,000 or so, I got nowhere with the idea of combining *Philolexian* and *Jester* and building an off-campus castle on the model of the Harvard *Lampoon*'s. It is still a wonderful idea, for both organizations have rich and eminent alumni. (Yes, I know *Philo* has lapsed.)

I have only one piece of advice for undergraduates: Do not even try to predict the success or failure in the big world of your classmates. I can testify that the effort is entirely futile, and perhaps pointless. But it is possible and useful to judge your peers on the qualities of talent, brains, and friendship. This latter is the data worth having.

Ideas and Poetry

⁂

by Louis Simpson

I don't know how she strikes others, but Alma Mater on the steps, one hand holding a scepter, the other turned palm upward, to me seems to be saying, "Don't blame me. It's your problem." She looks right through such quarrels as I have with my education, and says, "What did you expect? Poetry?"

My first and most powerful memory of Columbia is of being overwhelmed by the Humanities. Many have praised this course, and so do I, for I have seen places where nothing like it exists. Sheep being herded into a field—that's the so-called liberal arts college today. As critics such as Robert

---

LOUIS SIMPSON, *1949 General Studies, 1950 M.A., 1959 Ph.D., won the Pulitzer Prize for Poetry in 1964, the Columbia Medal for Excellence the next year. He was on the College faculty from 1956 to 1959, and has been at Berkeley since.*

Hutchins and William Arrowsmith have pointed out, it seems that the university, a place where you discover ideas, is vanishing, to be replaced by vocational training. But students at Columbia were exposed to ideas; in fact, some of us were encouraged not to settle down. In the Humanities, every Monday morning we were hurled into a new set of ideas, along with our instructors. Clutching one another, we tried to keep afloat. Ideas came pouring in; facts could be dealt with later.

One result of the course was that we liked ideas so well that we never got around to facts. When you had discussed the great ideas in the very best books, what could you possibly learn from experience? How could you give yourself to any one idea? And how could you ever write a research paper? In later years, the unfinished thesis was, in certain circles, a sign of the Columbia College man. In my travels I have come across the type, exiled from Columbia and condemned to live in the hinterland, because he had so many ideas that he could settle on none—at any rate, not long enough to write a thesis.

For my instructor in the Humanities I drew Lionel Trilling. Gracefully he led us from Homer to Spinoza to Fielding. His classes were chamber music in which we might be called upon to play a note or two. Then the bell rang and our conductor vanished. For me, it was like visions in a Chinese restaurant. There seemed to be an explanation, a clear reason for everything, but when I reached for it, it disappeared like a tail around a corner. I was too wrapped up in the words of the books I read to see that books are not just literature; they are part of something more important, the history of ideas, and most ideas are political. However, others saw the point, and some of my fellow students went on to become publishers, critics, and book reviewers:

hae tibi erunt artes; pacisque imponere morem,
parcere subiectis, et deballare superboe.

I did get a crack at just literature, in a course taught by Raymond Weaver. He had a brow overhanging a glare; his voice was deep and resonant. It was said that he had lived in Japan; he had "discovered" Herman Melville; he was an amateur boxer. It was Weaver's habit to make a dramatic entrance and ask a startling question. I'm still rather proud of an answer I gave. He asked, "What is Aristotle's *Art of Poetry* about?" and I said, "How to write a play." As was his custom if the answer was correct, he ignored it.

Weaver preferred the stolid, unimaginative type of student to those who were, like himself, rather aesthetic. In his repertoire he had a trick that underlined this prejudice. He would recite "Casey at the Bat":

Ten thousand eyes were on him as he rubbed his hands with
    dirt,
Five thousand tongues applauded when he wiped them on
    his shirt;
Then while the writhing pitcher ground the ball into his hip,
Defiance gleamed in Casey's eye, a sneer curled Casey's lip.

Then he recited Dowson's poem about Cynara:

I cried for madder music and for stronger wine,
But when the feast is finished and the lamps expire,

Then falls thy shadow, Cynara! the night in thine;
And I am desolate and sick of an old passion,
    Yea hungry for the lips of my desire:
I have been faithful to thee, Cynara! in my fashion.

Then he would ask which was poetry. Inevitably some poor
fish would bite, saying that "Cynara" was poetry and "Casey"
wasn't. Whereupon, in his booming voice Weaver would explain the pretentiousness of "Cynara," its insincerity, its essential vulgarity. Some years after witnessing this performance,
I met a man on Broadway who had had the misfortune to
choose "Cynara." He steered our conversation back to this
episode. He had been thinking about it for years, and thought
he had been right, and unjustly treated, and was thinking of
going to Weaver and telling him so. For all I know, he is
still there, on the corner of 116th Street, telling his side of
the story. But Weaver is not there. Had he lived to old age, I
think he would have been one of those grand academic men
of whom Wordsworth speaks, who give a university a druidic
aura, who cast terror and awe before them as they walk, and
leave a trail of humor in their wake. I do not see men like
this coming out of the present-day graduate schools.

And I did get to poetry, with Mark Van Doren. His way
of teaching was to talk about a book and express the thoughts
that came into his head. He seemed to be composing the book,
alongside Shakespeare, or Hardy, or Yeats. This was hardly a
method, but he filled us with enthusiasm. He made us feel
that we could write. Now, I am aware of the criticisms that
may be made of such teaching, but more and more I place
a high value on sympathy and enthusiasm in teaching, and a
low value on method. For a great deal of method, when you

examine it, is only another man's opinion tricked out with an apparatus. Of course, a teacher without a system must be in some way exemplary; he must have read much and be intelligent—or else his teaching is just sentimental. Van Doren was exemplary.

He put the finishing touch to my education. From then on, it was poetry that mattered. And if I have made my refusals— to be serious about scholarship, or editing, or writing criticism—it is because Van Doren encouraged me to think that poetry is more important than anything else. I have sometimes thought harshly of Columbia, because it is so conveniently near to the marketplace. As the creator of Marjorie Morningstar says, "At hand, as a quick change from the world of timeless values and hard intellectual work, was the wonderland of cynical, sophisticated New York." Cynicism and sophistication are the death of wonder, and the distance from Columbia to Madison Avenue is all too short. But whenever I am inclined to find fault with Columbia, I remember that Van Doren was part of it. There was poetry there, too, in those days.

Of Van Doren and Butler

by Carlos P. Romulo

When I entered the Graduate Faculties I was assigned to an adviser. This happened to be Professor Carl Van Doren. "So you come from the Philippines?" he said when I appeared in his office, "and you want to major in American literature?"

I informed him that in high school we read a bit, among others, of Longfellow, Poe, Thoreau, and Emerson.

"Then you must have read *Walden*."

CARLOS P. ROMULO *received his undergraduate degree from the University of the Philippines, of which he became president in 1962, and his M.A. in English from Columbia. He has served his native Philippines in scores of military, diplomatic, governmental, educational, and journalistic capacities, and has been president of the General Assembly of the United Nations.*

My answer, which was in the affirmative, signaled the beginning of a long dialogue on Walden Pond, Thoreau's ideas and American society of the period, broken only when he remembered that I had mentioned earlier the name of Emerson. We discussed then Emerson's essays, which he seemed to like nearly as well as Thoreau's, if not more.

"I think you should specialize on some particular aspect of American literature. How about current writers?" This was about 1919 and I mentioned the name O. Henry.

"That's good," Professor Van Doren said. "But what attracts you to O. Henry, his surprise endings?"

"Well then, see Mrs. Fisher at the library and get all the books by O. Henry you can find. Come back after a week or so."

Thus Professor Van Doren took me under his wing. I returned again and again to his office, consulted with him, literally sat at his feet, and so today my memories of Columbia are inextricably of Professor Carl Van Doren as well.

It was probably through him or from him that Dr. Nicholas Murray Butler learned about me. I not only made the acquaintance of Dr. Butler but became his friend so much so, that I dared invite him as a Rizal Day Speaker.

"I have read a lot about the Philippines," he said, and that was a fairly good sign of his sentiments toward the country. He was a Republican, was in fact a presidential possibility. I was amazed by his information not only about the Philippines but also of our educational system at that time. "There are eighteen million of you, and you have established a school system using English as the medium of instruction.

"You know, if only you had come earlier, you would have had your Rizal Day speaker, but, my dear young man, I have to go to Canada for a rest," he said. "If you had only given me two weeks notice." At this point he pressed the buzzer, and when his secretary arrived he asked that she produce a volume of congressional speeches that he kept on file.

"You see," he said, "I know a lot about José Rizal, your national hero," and, pulling out one of the items in the folder said, "Here is a speech for example in which Rizal's 'Last Farewell' was quoted on the floor of our House of Representatives. The speaker had thought it proper to defend the Philippines on the floor of Congress against the insinuations that your people are barbarians, so he quoted Rizal's 'Last Farewell' and he asked his audience, 'Now, gentlemen, would you say that a nation that can produce a poet like that is a nation of barbarians?' "

At about this time I was also reading Marx and Engels for a course in radical literature conducted by Professor Vladimir Simkhovitch, and in literary criticism I had Professor Brander Matthews, Professor Seligman in economics, and I attended the classes of Professor Carl Phlen, Dean Lawrence, Professor Ayres, and many others, all of whom I remember with profound gratitude. To all of these men, my debt is boundless.

Memoirs of
a Galley Slave

༈

by Paul Gallico

Daydreaming out of my picture window overlooking the
port of Antibes when I ought to be working, I see the four-
and eight-legged water spiders of the local rowing club, skit-
tering out of the harbor, the Mediterranean sun glinting from
their oars, and I cannot shut out the flood of memories of
my rowing days at Columbia a half century ago.

I watch the progress of the crews over the flat calm of the
Baie des Anges and wonder whether I could still sit up
properly in a boat, keep my slide under me, lay my back
into the oar, whip out the blade with a sharp snap of the

PAUL GALLICO, *1921 B.S., has been a movie critic, sports
writer, editor, and columnist, all for the New York* Daily
News, *a war correspondent for* Cosmopolitan, *and a free-
lance writer of fact and fiction for more than thirty years.*

wrist, and keep the shell running smoothly under me by pulling up on my toes. And how would it feel? And how long would I last?

How ancient the history seems at the time of my freshman crew in 1916. Woodrow Wilson was President of the United States and Jess Willard Heavyweight Champion of the World. As we took to our shells in the spring, the Brooklyn Dodgers and the Boston Red Sox were on their way to pennants. In the subsequent World Series, which Boston won, a pitcher by the name of George Herman Ruth chalked up a victory. A horse called, believe it or not, George Smith won the Kentucky Derby that year. Dick Williams and Molla Bjursted were to be respective tennis champions at Forest Hills, and there was also to be a considerable stir in golf. For the first time in the history of the game an amateur, Charles Evans, Jr., would win both the U. S. Open and Amateur championships, or just one half of the unrivaled grand slam scored by Bob Jones in 1930. The world's record for the mile run was still four minutes, twelve and six-tenths seconds, held by Norman Taber.

Of course World War I was in full spate, though we were not yet in it. That was to come in 1917. I had made the varsity that year. But when we entered the war in April, intercollegiate rowing was canceled. Thus my years of varsity competition were 1920 and 1921, preceded by a hitch in the Navy as a gunner's mate. The Navy, naturally. Where else would an oarsman go?

Unfathomable are the quirks of memory. Certain names, faces, and events are with me as clearly as though they had happened yesterday; others present a complete hiatus. In 1920 the intercollegiate regatta was held on Lake Cayuga at

Cornell University, at two miles. I remember nothing of it whatsoever; not where we trained or what the race was like, though the record book tells me we finished third to Syracuse and Cornell, beating only Pennsylvania.

Yet the hell of the 1921 regatta at Poughkeepsie is inextinguishable, for we thought we would win. It was my senior year and I was acting captain. During the night before the race the entire crew was up, trudging back and forth, to and from the latrine with diarrhea so severe that a Mickey Finn was suspected, though in all probability it was just plain ordinary food poisoning. None of the eight escaped. When we boated our shell the next day, we were as weak as mice. We finished a harrowing last.

We probably would never have won that year anyway, for it was Navy's first visit to Poughkeepsie. In practice they rowed at a constant clip of forty strokes to the minute. Our own racing tempo was to start at thirty-six, drop to twenty-eight for the long pull, and sprint at the finish. Navy was proposing to row the three miles at forty all the way. We weren't worried because we knew they were crazy and that it couldn't be done. But they weren't. And it could. And they did.

I had never meant to be an oarsman. I wanted to play football. Pure chance led me to encounter Jim Rice, the rowing coach, on the first day the winter of 1916 that I strode the campus as a freshman, before the football coach saw me. Both were on the prowl for big, rangy fellows.

Rice was a famous character and I nearly died of excitement when he stopped me, asked my name, age, and weight and whether I had ever rowed before, and then ordered me to report to the gymnasium that night for initial crew practice on the machines. Thrilled and flattered, it never occurred to me that I had any other choice but to obey. At that it was fortunate for me, for I was always a rotten football player, inclined to flinch. But I was able to carry out Rice's axiom for an oarsman, "You've got to be able to punish yourself." I could inflict endless brutalities upon myself; I just didn't like others to do it.

The Columbia boathouse then was a tumble-down, waterfront shack on the west bank of the Hudson, beneath what is now Palisades Park, and to get there after the day's classes we crossed by the old 135th Street ferry. The George Washington Bridge wasn't even on the planner's board. Fred Plaisted was the freshman coach. The boathouse keeper and rigger was an old, bad-tempered curmudgeon by the name of Pete, who used to chew on his teeth and make life as difficult as he could for the freshmen. He despised us and we hated him.

But first there were the winter days and the rowing machines set up in the gymnasium, three parallel sets of eight, with sliding seats and mechanical tension to the oars. There on dry land we learned the theories of keeping our slides under us, getting our backs into it, and, at the finish of the stroke, snapping the wrist, which one hoped would whip the blade cleanly out of the water. My ears still retain the "squeak-CHUNK, squeak-CHUNK, squeak-CHUNK" of all twenty-four machines in rhythmic action. Of course, when we went out onto the Hudson and for the first time sat in a barge with a twelve-foot oar it was all different, and we had to learn over again. And then once more, when we graduated to the paper-thin shell.

Jim Rice was a Canadian, a powerful, barrel-shaped man in his sixties, sardonic, ribald, and engagingly foul-mouthed. He subscribed to the then still popular cult of the he-man and would scornfully warn, "Now, I don't want to see any of you fellows playing that there game of long penis." From which we gathered that the sissy game of lawn tennis was not for stalwarts of the crew.

My ears somehow seem to remember as much of those days as my eyes, and I can still hear the long-drawn-out cry of Jim from the coaching launch, through his megaphone, between toots of tugs, ferryboats, and Central Railroad of New Jersey barges, "Gal-EEE-ko! You're feathering under. Sit up in the boat! You look like a greyhound frigging a wheelbarrow." This was one of his milder descriptions of my efforts.

The ancient boathouse there knew no amenities. There was only an icy shower into which to dash, hot and sweating from the pull. But one wonderful custom Rice introduced from his native Canada. He kept a cask of ale on tap, and at the end of practice we lined up and each oarsman received a glass—"To take the edge off," as Rice put it. No drink has ever tasted better to me than that draught of dark brown liquid at the finish of an eight- or ten-mile grind.

My place in the boat was port on Number 6 (at a pinch I could also handle starboard Number 7), known to the downtown papers as "the engine room of the boat." For we were all 180- and 190-pounders back there in the stern.

The downtown papers in those days seemed to take an extraordinary interest in rowing and gave me an embarrassing time with one sports page headline when, in a scuffle with a classmate on the library steps, I injured my right wrist. It read: "GALLICO, TOWER OF POWER, OUT OF VARSITY WITH INJURY." It took me more than a year to live down that "Tower of Power." It used to boom out through Rice's megaphone, "Come on Tower, let's see some of your goddamn power!"

I recall the slurping rustle of the water against the polished skin of our shell as, after the drive and the feather, eight of us sneaked forward on our slides to keep her running so that the stroke oar would dip again well behind the puddle left by the bow; the hoarse "Catch-drive!" of the coxswain and the clatter of his tiller handles on the side of the boat when he called for us to raise the stroke for a sprint. Then, the "'Way-all!" from the coaching launch, the momentary silence as we rested on oars, and then the expected trumpet from Jim Rice, "Gal-EEE-ko! You're shooting your tail! Keep your arse under you!" This meant that I wasn't pivoting properly, swinging against the firm anchorage of the blade in water, my bottom kept under the center of gravity to give full leverage for the stroke. There was more to rowing than just pulling, even though one of Jim's aphorisms was that his preference for an oarsman was a weak mind and a strong body. He had others too, such as his final command as we would draw away from the boathouse to head for the starting line of a race. It was "Don't get tired."

I did learn eventually, and happily never suffered that greatest of all oarsman's humiliations of catching a crab in a race, that is to say, losing control of my oar and breaking up the rhythm of the boat.

We were a spotty crew, fatigue-prone in the intercollegiates but occasionally winning one like the Child's Cup, or a dual match. Once we lured an aristocratic Princeton team up into the sewage of our Harlem River course and managed to pick our way through the vulgar and often mortifying flotsam and jetsam slightly more hurriedly than they.

But they got even. They invited us back to their Carnegie Lake, where they gave us a good trouncing. Nobody had warned us that this artificial bit of water, created through the munificence of Andrew Carnegie, was shallow and hence, believe it or not, slushy. We were accustomed to anchoring our blades in honest river fluid on which you could heave back with all your strength. Lake Carnegie's surface was like mush and we couldn't bite into it firmly with our oars. We felt as though we were rowing in soapsuds.

Why do I remember no more than ten or so of my crew mates, and not others? Or in what boat they were, or when, and what has become of them?

I would not be likely to forget Dunc Leys, the varsity stroke, and my boyhood hero when I was a freshman. He was a lanky, lantern-jawed, self-possessed athlete. I was also afraid of him, though he never gave me cause to be. But the relationship between freshmen and upper classmen was then still one of juvenile terrorism. Perhaps it still is today. I rowed Number 7 behind his stroking beat, bursting with pride in 1917, until as noted the war broke up our schedule. When I returned to college in 1920 to complete my education he was, of course, gone and there seemed to be a whole new crowd, with only one or two exceptions.

There was Kess Scovil, a doctor's son, my particular pal, and we were inseparable. Our stroke in the postwar years was a tough and irreverent athlete by the name of Frank Brodil. He was not built like an oarsman, but rather like the well-known brick you-know-what, with a sense of humor that was wanting in some of the more refined attitudes toward intercollegiate competition. I remember one time, when we were pulling away from Yale on the Housatonic— much to our surprise—our stern drew level with Yale's bowman, who happened to be a scion of one of the reigning socialite families. This was Sonny Whitney, whose wife, I note, had $780,000 worth of her baubles heisted at Saratoga last summer. Brodil baited him by calling across, "Hey, Whitney, what time is it?"

Two of our bowmen stick in my mind, one by the name of Horace Dow, who was notable in that he had once been a Broadway chorus boy, but with none of the implications inherent in that kind of work. The theater was just entering its glamor period then and some of it must have surrounded him. The other, a chap named Ruffalo, was one of those tough *paisanos* with a beak like an octopus and rather the same kind of eyes. He was, of course, nicknamed Tito because of an opera singer then current by the name of Titta Ruffo. He seemed to come in for a good deal of kidding. Lansing Van Houten was our captain in 1921, a big, blond boy who looked like the Arrow collar man. Ads for Arrow collars in those days were drawn by an artist named Leyendecker, and that was just about as handsome as you could get. He had the misfortune to go down with pneumonia before the intercollegiates, which moved me into the position of acting captain.

This was essentially the same crew that contributed to what must have been one of the silliest sights in all rowing history. We were at Annapolis for a dual meet with the Navy and had gone out in the morning to try to get used to the choppy waters of the Severn. We had splashboards on our shell, but the wind kicked up rougher and rougher until we gradually filled and quietly sank. But since our eight oars— four on a side—were kept out at right angles, we didn't tip over but merely descended, so that eight nude torsos emerged from the water, one behind the other. Of the cox, only his head was visible. His name was Don Brush. He had reddish hair, crew-cut, of course, an impertinent face, and a highly irritating voice.

I don't know how it is today, probably football has supplanted crew in importance, but then we were the aristocrats of the campus. For we were letter men plus, and wore the block "C" with crossed oars, the highest athletic award. To walk the campus wearing the dark blue crew hat sporting this emblem in white embroidery made one feel lordly. There was much sacrifice, discipline, and physical torture connected with being a crewman, but it was worth every bit of it to be able to sport that hat, or peacock in a big white sweater with the insignia in light blue. Of all that happened to me at Columbia, including my degree, I suspect that winning my letter was the most important and gave me the most satisfaction. My vanity must have been overweening.

The races were sheer nightmares. And I remember that, several times during the worst of them, when my chest was on fire, I could not get any air into my lungs, with my arms and legs ready to drop off, I would despair of pulling another ten strokes when I knew there were yet several hundred ahead of me. I would wonder then how I ever had come to let myself in for such a painful sport.

I can see it only as an anguish from start to finish. For from the moment the gun went off and one heaved into the starting sprint at thirty-eight to forty strokes a minute, one began to gasp for breath and never really caught it again, never felt easy or in control or out of misery the full length of the course.

Added to this was the humiliation of seeing rival crews pulling away and knowing that trying to catch them would only bring on an increase of physical agony. Being last, finding ourselves practically alone on the river, did nothing to assuage the awful discomfort of having to go pulling on until one crossed the finish line and collapsed over one's oars. The members of the winning crew, of course, never collapsed. It was strange, too, how sometimes we managed to do some of our most beautiful rowing on the way back to the boathouse after a defeat.

But against this was the enchantment of the long practice spins on the Hudson to the north and south of our training camp at Poughkeepsie; mornings and afternoons of warm spring days on a placid river. Here we became one with the boat and our fellow oarsmen and felt ourselves as giants, since one's own power applied to the shell was multiplied by eight. Not often, but from time to time, there are moments when a good crew really blends together, bringing an ineffable delight to the rower as he feels his shell surge forward beneath him. Eight oars whip out of the water in unison; eight oars dip again and one feels a great exultation in one's breast.

But there was yet another reward for the hardships connected with a season of rowing and that was the three-week training session at Poughkeepsie at the end of the spring term and prior to the intercollegiate regatta. There again on the west bank of the Hudson we had our own stone boathouse, a fine

new one, with dormitories on the second floor. Three crews—
varsity, junior varsity, and freshman—lived and trained together, at the same time indulging in some of the strange
anthropological rituals arising in all-male societies. One of
these included the paddling of freshmen as a part of the Saturday night's amusement. We were required to put on songs,
dances, or playlets to entertain the upper classmen and, having
done this, were then taken out to the back porch, commanded
to "Bend ovah," and then were struck on our behinds five or
six times with a heavy wooden paddle with all the force that
could be mustered by a 185-pound athlete.

I never understood this quite. Considering that the next
morning we would be required to pivot on those same bruised
buttocks during an eight- or nine-mile training spin, it did
not seem too clever.

Yet they were wonderful days of cohesive and cooperative
effort, particularly when I returned as an upper classman after
the war; a long walk in the morning before breakfast, another
at night before retiring, good food, steaks galore, friendship,
and the mounting tension as race day approached.

No matter, we were all far more innocent, uncluttered, and
uncomplicated than now, and I wouldn't have had it any
different. But I am just as pleased now to be watching the
efforts of the young Frenchmen flashing their blades in and
out of the Bay of the Angels, while I enjoy the sweet ease
of retrospect.

A Stranger
to the Law

༃⚜⚜⚜༃

by William O. Douglas

I reached Morningside Heights after a long ride on a freight
train across the country from Yakima, Washington. The East
was entirely new to me and at first blush vastly different from
the warm and friendly western communities where I grew
up. I was, moreover, without resources, and in those days
there were no scholarship loans or grants. And I had no
friend, companion, or confidant to whom to turn. I mention
these facts only to indicate how lonesome and bewildered I
was when I entered Kent Hall that September morning.

WILLIAM O. DOUGLAS, *1925 Law, taught law at Columbia
from 1925 to 1928, has sat as Associate Justice of the Supreme Court of the United States since 1939, and, among
many books, has written accounts of high adventure in the
Orient, the Middle East, the American West, the Soviet Union, and other places.*

My first class was Contracts, the professor being Herman Oliphant—medium height, piercing eyes, and clipped speech. He succeeded Charles T. Terry, professor of note. This was Oliphant's first class at Columbia; and I later learned when I joined him on the faculty that he was tense and nervous and as much on edge as the attendant who enters a lion's cage. But this morning he was to me the symbol of "the Law," with all its severity.

There was a seat assignment for the class; and I sat on the aisle in the sixth row from the front. The room was packed with 365 students, every seat taken. Promptly at nine o'clock, Oliphant entered, placed his casebook and notes on the table on the lectern, pursed his lips, and wiped his spectacles with a handkerchief while the entire group remained so silent one could hear a pin drop.

After cleaning his eyeglasses, Oliphant left the lectern and passed through the room walking slowly up one side aisle and down the center aisle. It was a slow, funereal walk, as I told him years later, and not a word was uttered. I could hear his measured steps coming down the center aisle and soon my worst fears were realized. He stopped by my side and asked me to stand up, which of course I did. After asking me my name, he put the grin of a Cheshire cat on his face and said in a loud voice:

"Mr. Douglas, please tell the class what an estoppel is."

My mind was blank, for I did not recall ever having heard the word before. I stood in silence for a moment. Oliphant spoke up, "Come, please tell us."

I replied that I did not have the faintest idea what an estoppel was.

Turning to the class he asked, "Will those who know what an estoppel is, please raise your hands?"

A dozen eager hands went up—and my heart sank. For I had the awful feeling that "the law," wholly strange to me, would be my nemesis.

Three and a Half Years
at Columbia

꘎꘎꘎꘎꘎

by John Berryman

Those lost years.

Two things never faltered: my arrogance, and the need to sit at the feet of exceptional men.

I remember Dean Hawkes powdered with chalk dust as he wrestled with the blackboard teaching Solid Geometry—so ably that, ever since, my sense of volumes and relations has been an active part of my observation. This was in my last year, to wind up a science requirement that I had got behind with when I skipped the sixth form at South Kent, taking boards and entering Columbia from the fifth form. I knew

JOHN BERRYMAN, *1936 College, has graced the faculties of Wayne, Harvard, and Princeton, among others. His poetry has won many prizes and his literary criticism has appeared in many publications.*

the Dean quite well by this time. Our acquaintance began in my freshman year; one morning there arrived in the mail a letter saying that the Dean wanted to see me at my earliest convenience. "Well, that's damned nice of the Dean," I said to myself. "I really must drop in and see the old boy some time." Several more of these letters came, and had no further effect than the first. Then came a telephone call from his secretary, stating that unless I arrived in his office before noon that day I would be suspended. Our interview was friendly but stern: unless I cut down on my extracurricular activities and stopped cutting classes, Columbia was obviously not for me. The Dean seemed to be horribly well informed about those activities—how, I don't know to this day. They were chiefly three in number: sports (track and crew), social life (mostly with Barnard), and politics (Tom McGovern, Paul Mac-Cutched, and myself, tied of the hegemony of the fraternities, created an Independent Party, which after two years had a majority on the Student Council; even as freshmen we captured two of the four class posts, myself losing the vice-presidency by just five votes to an Alpha Delt from Kent). I fell foul of the Dean's office in other ways too, and was a familiar figure there by the time, at the end of my sophomore year, I flunked a course, losing my scholarship, and the Dean told me gently that it might be well if the College and I parted company for a while, to give me a chance to think things over. That is to say, I was thrown out. To cut this story short, when I performed in a very different way during my last year and a half I became even more noticeable to that sweet man Dean Hawkes and he headed my way everything he legitimately could—Phi Beta Kappa, the Kellett for two years at the University of Cambridge—and he also barely saved my life just before graduation, a story I'll tell presently.

A word about that flunked course. It was Mark Van Doren's Eighteenth Century. I wrote an excellent final, but because Mark and I were already very friendly I put a note at the end saying that of the forty-two books in the course I had read only seventeen. He wrote a note below mine saying how well he liked the exam and my candor, but he would have to flunk me in view of my admission. This was a heavy blow to me in many ways, most in the feeling that I had let him down. So I sat down for some months reading all the forty-two books in the course and keeping a notebook on them that ran to several hundred pages, including a thirty-page digest of Locke's *Essay*, which Mark said later ought to be published, only we found that someone else had done one. Anyway, at last one day I handed him the vast manuscript, hoping that it would repair our friendship. To my amazed delight it did even more. He was impressed and showed it to the Dean and they agreed to change my mark in the course and restore my scholarship and welcome me back to the College. This is not the only time in my life that I have been snatched back from the edge of the abyss, nor the only time a grade was changed—as I'll tell you later.

I remember circling and circling and circling South Field with Plochmann after Colloquium each week, thrashing through again the arguments of Kant and Freud, criticizing the two masters of the Colloquium (a musician-philosopher and an economist), and tearing to shreds our colleagues the thirteen other undergraduates.

I remember Professor Casey, the chief spellbinder of Columbia in my time—and not in my time only, for I read recently with satisfaction that he had received a high award, a gold medal or something, for distinguished teaching; that's thirty years later, a long time, and no award was ever more deserved. His course was called, I believe, Sociology 3–4, and its materials were conventional enough (Vaihinger's *Philosophy of the As If,* Wittgenstein, Lippman's *The Phantom Public,* and so on). But his lectures had nothing to do either with sociology (whatever that may be) or with the texts assigned. He would walk into the lecture room, jammed like Grand Central, a tall lean remote figure with a large white handkerchief drooping from his coat pocket, look over us out the high windows, and then in fifty minutes destroy some subject. "Today," he would say, "we'll take up the League of Nations problem"—that is to say, why the United States never joined it, and all of us would rub our hands together with *Schadenfreude:* during the coming hour we would hear The Word and could go torture our other instructors with it. There were no questions, no discussion; it was said that Casey had never looked directly even at his assistant. At one point in the League of Nations lecture, I remember he took from his pocket a letter and opened it and said, "I have here a letter from a farmer in Wisconsin, who has heard that the Prince of Wales is often thrown from his horse" (hence we never entered the League). Now a Wisconsin farmer would cut little ice at the university, Minnesota, where I now mostly teach, but on 116th Street he looks powerful indeed: grass roots. He never quoted anything except from private letters and from a pulp magazine called *The Shadow,* and as far as I know never read anything else; his correspondence was world-wide and produced a marvelous vividness in the lecture room. It was a superb show, and I hit it at exactly the right time, as a sophomore: if I had come on it later, I would have missed the enthusiasm, the glee of destruction, whereas if I had had it as a freshman I might have been taken in for longer. For instance, one of his masterpieces was an attack on Keats' *Ode to a Grecian Urn*. I was enchanted with this, my first acquaintance with logical positivism, but immediately saw that it was nonsense and moved from Casey on to more reliable guides.

I remember Raymond Weaver, the American discoverer of Melville, a man with a massive voice and presence. He was fond of two things: unannounced hour examinations and academic jokes. (I speak only of his teaching, he did other things as well). One day he walked into our classroom on the third floor of Hamilton and boomed, "Write me out the first canto of the *Inferno* in the style of Homer, and bring it down to my office." I spent half an hour at this and went down to his office. "Put it there," he said, "there" being his wastepaper basket. His marking must have been the Dean's despair: only if he actively disliked you did he give you an A minus. One of his tales I recall as if it were yesterday. A Christian army is investing a pagan city, when at the last moment a lieutenant rides up to the captain and says, "Captain, there are some Christians in this city. How shall we know them from the pagans?" *"Kill 'em all!* Christ will know his own."

I remember the coaches (except, by some blockage, the track coach, who in a meet made me run both the quarter-mile—worst of all distances—and the half-mile) with affection and respect: the younger Glendon, the swimming coach who said to me one afternoon, "Berryman, you get through the water faster with less style than anyone I have ever tried to teach," and Gus in wrestling who, to prove to everybody that the human neck is much stronger than it appears, had me get down on all fours and delivered the rest of his harangue sitting on my neck. I also remember the gay regatta day when my sliding seat lodged under my legs during the racing start and I rowed the whole race on the runners, winding up a mass of torn chamois and blood.

I remember Irwin Edman's undergraduate seminar in metaphysics. It met once a week in his apartment and one had to endure some of Brahms' chamber music first, and there were usually one or two learned sailors present, but we read the whole of Plato in chronological order and this was one of the most important experiences I had as an undergraduate, along with reading the whole of Shakespeare in chronological order under Mark Van Doren. (On the other hand, I graduated without having read either the Bible or Cervantes.) Edman tended to treat Socrates and Plato a little as if they were Santayana, but was otherwise good at exposition and a pleasant man, although he once read two of my lousy poems to a large lecture audience as "philosophical poetry." This I never forgave him for, and I still owe him a paper on Santayana's literary psychology but do not know his address, for he is dead.

I remember, for paralyzing dullness, an emeritus from Cornell on the History of the Ancient Orient, a history that consisted solely of reign and battle dates. I took care with my examination because I wanted an A, but then I risked it by turning in, instead of a term paper, a long poem on Egyptian religion, a little matter he had failed to mention in lecture; to my amazement he gave it an A too.

I remember, as proof of definite idiocy on my part, that I never took anything with either Meyer Schapiro or Lionel Trilling.

I remember a freak event which taught me something about the aleatory element in human experience. Dana Crandall and I were returning to our rooms on the sixth floor of John Jay very late one night, when I unlocked my door, switched on the overhead, and—wham—I went out like a light. Luckily, Crandall heard me fall, came in and got me to, and took me down Amsterdam to the hospital, where I was treated for shock and had my head wound dressed. I woke up next morning burning with rage and complained bitterly to the Dean's office. I was prominent enough on campus to have many enemies and we assumed that one of them had slugged me. But there was a problem: where had he been and where had he gone? Not out the window, which was two floors above the roof over the entrance to John Jay; there was nowhere in the room to hide; Crandall, just a few feet away, had a full view of the hall. All we had to go on was an empty whiskey bottle on the floor under my bed, which might have caused the wound, but how was it wielded? It was days before the Dean called me in and told me what had happened (how he found out God knows and I forget): a drunken student out on the entrance roof had finished his bottle and hurled it upward and backward over his shoulder and the damned thing came sailing through my open window at the precise instant when I entered the room: pure accident.

I remember my twenty-first birthday party, when a classmate, one of my closest friends, took my girl up to the roof of my apartment building on 115th Street and kept her there hours. The later history of this man is interesting. The next time I saw him he was a Roman Catholic priest with a parish in New York. The last time I saw him was when he called my hotel in Chicago to tell me that he had left the

Church and become a radio announcer; we met and had an awkward drink.

I remember the general excitement of running things in my senior year: Philolexian, Boar's Head, and, with Bob Giroux, *The Columbia Review*, which we made practically professional.

This slight reminiscence of Columbia has both a hero and a villain.

The villain was named Neff and he tried to keep me from graduating. I cannot do him justice in a short space but I will try. He taught the Nineteenth Century and a worse teacher I have never known. Even Professor Schmidt of Cornell did no active harm, he was only pointless, whereas Professor Neff, with his mouthing of Wordsworth, held up my appreciation of that great poet for a whole year; he taught the vile Carlyle with enthusiasm; he informed us that Swinburne was the last of the great poets. He was a great ass, in short, and when his marks were finally posted I had a C. I had been prepared for trouble with Neff (that is, a B) because I had made a perfect hell of his life all year, and I had followers—we were not disrespectful, merely ironic. But I was not prepared for a C, which meant that I could not graduate. Let me explain. For every six credits of A, you get an extra credit, *provided* that you have no mark below B. I was carrying seven courses, twenty-one credits, and had A in my six other courses, giving me the three extra credits I needed to graduate (remember that I had been out of College for half a year) *if* Neff had given me a B. I learned that Neff had sailed for Europe, and I raised hell. Not only the Dean but everybody down through the English Department and Philosophy (my minor) was profoundly embarrassed that I could not graduate. They held meetings. It seemed hopeless, but gradually certain anomalies emerged for consideration. My six A's were very hard on his C, implausible. Second, Neff (we learned) had left instructions with his assistant to post his marks at the last possible moment, whereas seniors' marks are required by custom to be posted at once, as soon as possible; this made a bad impression on everybody. And third, I had an enormous notebook on all the readings in the course—not on the lectures, which were contemptible, but on the books read, and it did not look like a C notebook (whether I made this as insurance, or was simply lucky, I don't now remember). Still, to change the mark of a full professor in his absence seemed out of the question—until it seemed to be in various canvassings the only thing to try, and so it was decided to give me a second examination. I never learned what my grade was on it, but the course mark was changed to a B and I graduated. I had a nervous breakdown from overwork and spent the summer in Canada until I sailed for England.

The hero, of course, is Mark Van Doren. I hardly know what to say of him here. I took every course he gave, and from my sophomore year onward he was the presiding genius of all my work until my senior year, when I fell under the spell of W. B. Yeats. It is hard to describe teaching, but of Mark's teaching a good sense can be had in his books *Shakespeare* and *The Noble Voice*. It had nothing rhetorical about it, unless we think of paradox as rhetorical (which of course it is). It was strongly structured, lit with wit, leaving ample play for grace and charm. Common sense played a strong part in it; it was not at all like what one might suppose a poet's teaching to be, but rather like Father Hopkins's attack on Wordsworth ("The child is father to the man"). It stuck steadily to its subject and was highly disciplined. After thirty years I still recall with pain one moment. It was early in the Shakespeare course and we had reached some comparatively tiresome play, like *The Two Gentlemen of Verona* or *1 Henry VI*. He began the hour with a question, which the student called on could not answer, nor could the next student, nor the next. Then he asked how many of us had read the play. Two or three hands went up, of a class of thirty, and he closed his book without a word, walked to the door, and went out, while we sat stunned. Nobody moved for a long time, as we digested our shame. Nothing like that ever happened again. One of the reasons teaching is so hard to describe is because it is so closely bound up with the ideas of loyalty and personal distinction. If during my stay at Columbia I had met only Mark Van Doren and his work, it would have been worth the trouble. It was the force of his example, for instance, that made me a poet.

Some Recollections
of Great Teachers

by Clifton Fadiman

In the second century of our era, while resting in the course of his arduous campaigns against the German barbarians, the Roman emperor Marcus Aurelius set down his famous *Meditations*. My favorite passages are contained in the opening Book, in which he offers up thanks to those teachers who in his youth arranged for him to grow not into a mere emperor but into Marcus Aurelius.

If a cat may look at a king, an essayist may ape an em-

CLIFTON FADIMAN, *1925 College, has been known widely and well in radio, television, books, articles, essays, comments, and criticisms. A version of this essay appeared in* Holiday *in 1958 and was reprinted in* Enter, Conversing *(World Publishers, 1962), and is offered here by permission of both.*

peror. In this one respect I match myself with Marcus Aurelius: though the results are not comparable, I too have had good teachers, and perhaps three or four great ones. That this realization should strike me forcibly thirty-odd years after my graduation from Columbia is not strange, any more than it was strange for Marcus Aurelius to record his gratitude in his fifties. It takes at least a couple of decades for a man to discover that he was well taught. All true education is a delayed-action bomb, assembled in the classroom for explosion at a later date. I had a friend who, dying well and nobly, told me he drew his courage from something his philosophy teacher had said three decades before. And so an education fuse over thirty years long is by no means unusual.

Professor Mark Van Doren taught me English at Columbia long ago; and, as he is still talking and writing, though retired, he is still educating me, free of charge. When I try to think of what he taught me I cannot remember a thing. That is as it should be. The catalogue stated that he taught English. A catalogue however is not composed by teachers but by administrators who are fit for such chores. Mr. Van Doren of course taught English in the sense that he did not teach mathematics; but his real subject was one on which no examination could test you: human life. Mr. Van Doren is a poet, that rare being in whom passion and repose carry on a peaceful coexistence. In the classroom he never denied his vocation; he remained the poet, the poet as teacher. He taught us something simple, profound, sensible, and useful: that human life is enhanced if one can manage to see it with the imagination. There lay his subject, which the catalogue would label "Shakespeare" or "The Epic" or some other brand name.

In a way the great teacher—even the great mathematics

teacher—does not teach anything quantitatively measurable. He performs certain actions, says certain things that create *another* teacher. This other teacher is the one hidden inside the student. When the master teacher is finished, the newborn professor inside the student takes over, and with any luck the process of education continues till death. "The object of teaching a child is to enable him to get along without his teacher," said Elbert Hubbard. This capacity, rather than acquired information, marks the legacy of the great teacher.

The great teacher, one might add, is rarely "popular." He is interested in something more important than winning the affections of an unending anonymous procession of young people. The "beloved" teacher image is part of our American sentimental mythology: it expresses our willingness to pay homage to education provided it be painless—that is, non-educational. I have long maintained that any college can raise its standards simply by firing annually that professor voted "Best Liked" by the graduating class.

Mr. Van Doren did not waste his valuable time by interesting himself in us as individuals. He was willing to leave this job to Mamma and Papa. The great teacher does not bother to "love" or "understand" his students; he bothers to love their minds and understand their understandings. Mr. Van Doren did this by indirection. He reached us by paying attention, not to our trivial personalities, but to his subject and to the play of his own mind over his subject. He has put it thus: "The teacher whose love of truth is personal, is his own, is the teacher all students dream of encountering someday."

You will remember Socrates' demonstration, in Plato's *Meno,* that an illiterate slave boy can prove the Pythagorean

Theorem. It's just a question of education—that is, of *educing* the proof from the boy by asking the proper questions. All great teachers are smaller Socrateses. You may recognize them as much by what you say to them as by what they say to you.

So with Mr. Van Doren. In his classes it was quite easy to be a poor student—that is, vulnerable to an examination— but it was harder to be a poor human being. He had then, and has retained, this curious faculty of making you say things you would swear were far beyond your mental capacity. Possibly he does not know to this day why he has always found human beings more interesting than they really are.

The secret of course lies in the fact that no great teacher is democratic, in the sense that a successful politician must be. Mr. Van Doren calmly assumed a class composed entirely of heavy thinkers. At first this was embarrassing, for even in those days intellectuality and venereal disease enjoyed about equal prestige. After a while, however, you got used to it, and pretty soon you found yourself saying something almost publishable. I can remember philosophy classes, presided over by another fine teacher, Irwin Edman, in which football heroes suddenly, if transiently, became adults simply because Edman refused to treat them as anything else. Memorable is that quick look of panic mingled with amazed delight that would spread over their pleasant blank faces at the realization that they had given birth to an idea. By this look you may know that education is in process.

I have implied that the great teacher in a sense has no "department." I will go further. He may be unaware of what he is teaching. I once spent a year learning something from one of the finest teachers of my acquaintance, Harrison Ross Steeves, now retired. The something I learned was not what he taught—in fact, I cannot remember even the name of the course. Mr. Steeves was an extraordinarily handsome person (he looked a little like a less aquiline Sherlock Holmes) with a carriage of such elegant rectitude that he would have improved our minds if he had done nothing but stand up straight for fifty minutes. From the mouth of this naturally aristocratic being there flowed, in lecture after lecture, a clear stream of the purest and most beautifully organized informal oral English prose that I have ever heard. Week after week he taught us, whatever his titular subject may have been, respect for our English tongue. He did this merely by speaking perfectly; by assuming that beautiful speaking manners were preferable to ordinary ones; by treating each sentence, minute after minute, year after year, not as a passing jumble of vocables but as a small work of art. Since that classroom experience I happen to have made speaking part of my trade. Whatever trivial proficiency I have laboriously acquired is in part due to Mr. Steeves; in fact, I have been making a living out of him for years. He taught me and others to be ashamed of maltreating our magnificent English tongue. To implant that shame in perhaps fifteen thousand young men is a vast educational achievement.

I can think of at least one more mark of the great teacher. He often gains his best effects, not by iteration, not even by conscientious, steady pedagogy, but by strokes of lightning. The catalogue will say that he offers a year's course. But it may be as true to say that he offers a few magic moments. The teachers we remember are those who suddenly set our minds on fire, and perhaps did so no more than a single time.

The late Oscar Hammerstein II, speaking of John Erskine (another of my few unforgettable teachers), once recalled, "I attended his classes in 1916, and one day John read a poem. It came to me with a shock that poetry was intended to mean something. Whatever I've done in the theater I really owe to the way he read that poem."

The late James Newman, the brilliant editor of the now classic anthology *The World of Mathematics,* once told Professor Scott Buchanan (who also did his best to teach me greatly) that a few words Buchanan had dropped in an evening class many years ago had started Newman's life-long preoccupation with mathematics. It is notable, not only that Buchanan imparted to Newman this shock of recognition, but did so in the course of teaching not mathematics but philosophy—another evidence of the subordinate position occupied in the mind of the great teacher by his "specialty."

At the moment there are three orders of men at work in the American classroom: custodians, instructors, teachers.

The custodian is hired by the state to guard our children for five or six hours a day until they are ready to be thrown on the labor or marriage market. Because we are not happy with the sound of the preceding sentence, we give the custodian the name of teacher, often after he has completed courses guaranteed to prevent him from becoming one. Then we are shocked to discover that the custodian's connection with education is minimal. Quite unfairly we attack him for doing precisely the job we taxpayers have hired him to do: involve our children in busy work so that they will not add to the burden of either the patrolman or the juvenile deliquency officer. The custodian is the necessary, inevitable, and perfectly guiltless consequence of a society that prefers multiplication to the multiplication table.

The instructor, on the other hand, will remain indispensable as long as a fairly large number of Americans believe that the tools of learning must be put into the hands of our young people. He is master of a specific subject, or sometimes several subjects. His job is to siphon learning out of his superior mind into the student's inferior one. Provided he obeys the rules of decent morality and good citizenship, it is not essential that he possess qualities beyond this special ability.

Should he possess them he may turn out to be that invaluable rarity, the teacher, perhaps even the great teacher.

The custodian teaches nothing, though he may put a class through a series of exercises that have a shadowy resemblance to the educational process. The instructor teaches a subject. The teacher seems to teach a subject but is really engaged in doing a number of other things at the same time. We may define him as a human animal specialized to think in public, to think in public before anyone, but particularly before young people who have not as yet learned even to think in private. He is an exhibitionist, willing, even eager, to do an important part of his living, at stated intervals, for atrocious pay, before rows of plastic intellects.

The custodian keeps the student's body from getting into trouble. The instructor furnishes the student's mind. The teacher moves that mind. That movement, multiplied over time and space, adds up to a sum. The sum is civilization.

The Unloosened Mind

༂ৄᡰᡰᢀ᛫

by Paul H. Douglas

I came down to Columbia after graduating from Bowdoin in 1913 and enrolled as a graduate student in the Department of Economics, where I worked primarily under Edwin R. A. Seligman and Henry R. Seager. Most of the older professors in the Graduate Faculties of History, Political Science, and Economics had been trained in the German universities and this section of the graduate school was really modeled on

PAUL H. DOUGLAS *has his undergraduate degree from Bowdoin, his M.A. and Ph.D. from Columbia. A professor at Reed College, University of Washington, University of Chicago, Amherst, and the New School for Social Research, he has been adviser to a host of governmental bodies, and active in a political life which took him from Fifth Ward alderman in Chicago to the United States Senate.*

the University of Berlin. The emphasis was on the dissertation and the oral examination for the Ph.D. degree with no pressure to take examinations in specific courses.

Like all city universities where the lecture method was emphasized, there was not much personal contact between staff and students. Seligman and Seager were kindly men who tried to be friendly and helpful, but there was an inevitable air of impersonality around Kent Hall and the dormitories which made life seem cold to the student from a small college. Perhaps, however, it was a useful preparation for formal entrance into an impersonal world.

Seligman was an immensely learned man and the library and study in his home on West Eighty-sixth Street, where he held his seminars, was an inspiring place. He seemed to have read and to own every book and pamphlet written on economics, and particularly on public finance, before 1850.

Seager was an urbane scholar and an active participant in the movement for social insurance. I derived inspiration and information from him which was very valuable to me during the next three decades when I was working on many of these same problems.

But perhaps the greatest inspiration came from men outside the department, notably John Dewey, Charles A. Beard, and James T. Shotwell.

Beard was at the height of his powers and was the finest university lecturer I have ever heard. Every one of his lectures was a finished performance and threw new light on past events. I can especially remember his lecture on the Dred Scott decision which clearly indicated Buchanan's knowledge of what the decision was to be and possibly his connivance in its contents.

John Dewey was also at his very best and his lecture on the influence of Darwin on philosophical thought furnished me with an approach to life which I have never forgotten. I can also remember his treatment of the question whether the end justified the means. "Of course this is true," he said. "What else could justify them?" "But," he went on, "those who use this argument find that means commonly also become ends and are self-perpetuating." Similarly, drawing on his previous work at the University of Chicago and his path-breaking book *School and Society,* he would utter aphorisms, the full significance of which would gradually expand in my thought. One of these was "It is not we who think; rather it is thought which happens within us." And another, "The school is not a preparation for life. It is life itself."

Dewey unloosened our minds and gave us an experimental attitude toward life dominated by human and social values. I later came to know him quite well and I have always regarded him as one of the noblest men America has produced.

Shotwell was immensely stimulating in his treatment of the Industrial Revolution and gave me insights and knowledge later expanded by Peter Gay at Harvard.

But New York City itself was the great laboratory and teacher. The New Freedom of Wilson was coming into being. John Purroy Mitchel defeated Tammany in the mayoral election of 1913. The I.L.G.W.U. and the Amalgamated Clothing Workers were organizing the clothing workers and beginning the long battle to eliminate the sweatshop. The great New York *World* and the *Evening Post* were in their prime. Our F.P.A. had brought the column to New York. Greenwich Village was full of young and earnest men and women whose discussion and ardor were electric. Bernard Shaw's plays were at last on Broadway and were making a big hit. H. G. Wells, John Galsworthy, and John Masefield were the writers of the day. Here I discovered Tolstoy and later Dostoevsky and Turgenev. And in cheap restaurants and occasional saloons we graduate students would discuss the issues and controversies of that churning period.

I felt, as Wordsworth did a century before, "Bliss was it in that dawn to be alive, But to be young was very heaven."

I remember an evening in an outdoor restaurant on 110th Street and Riverside Drive when we talked the whole night through. Then in 1914 the age of innocence died and war came to the world. It has been different ever since.

So while Columbia did not give me any systematic drill in economic theory, it opened new doors, encouraged new interest and a humane attitude toward life. And perhaps in the long, long run, this was more important.

T.C. in the Thirties

⋟⋟⊹⊹⋞⋞

by Norman Cousins

It would be difficult to think of a school in the mid-thirties more drenched with a sense of living history than Teacher's College. Scarcely an issue involving civil liberties or human values in general would arise anywhere without reverberations at T.C. Some examples:

In 1935, when a cafeteria worker by the name of Manuel Romero was dismissed because he joined a food worker's union, many students exploded with rage and didn't let up

NORMAN COUSINS *studied at Columbia Teacher's College in a tumultuous time. He is well into his third decade as pilot of the* Saturday Review. *The subtitle of his latest book,* Present Tense, An American Editor's Odyssey, *accurately describes his life in a world of problems running from air pollution to the Hiroshima Maidens.*

until a student-faculty committee was created to look into the problem. The committee recommended that Mr. Romero be restored to his job, which he was.

In September 1935, Harold G. Campbell, superintendent of schools in New York City, dismissed eighty-five WPA playschool teachers for participating in a civil liberties demonstration. The issue exploded on the T.C. campus. Characteristically, George Counts led the T.C. attack on Superintendent Campbell.

In October 1935, Massachusetts was one of the first states to pass a loyalty oath law for teachers. Before the year was out, twenty-two states had similar laws on the books. T.C. faculty and students didn't wait for New York to be hit. George Counts and Goodwin Watson attracted national attention when they supported Professor Kirtley Mather of Harvard in his opposition to the legislation. Whether in classes or corridors, T.C. faculty and students were deeply agitated over the issue.

In December 1935, a "flag act" was proposed which would make mandatory the display of the American flag at all public meetings. Many T.C. stduents thought the proposed law was ludicrous and would make a mockery of patriotism by emphasizing its superficial manifestations.

In January 1936, T.C. students booed the head of the ROTC right off the campus.

In February 1936, when the first meeting of the John Dewey Society was held in St. Louis, William Kilpatrick, Goodwin Watson, and George Counts were the prime movers in getting the group to pass a resolution denouncing efforts to require teachers and administrators to take oaths to support the Constitution. The effect of the loyalty oaths, the resolution declared, was not so much to uphold the Constitution as it was to deprive students and teachers of their basic rights under the Constitution.

In 1936, stories appeared in newspapers about Eskimo children's difficulty in learning English. T.C. classes buzzed with controversy over ways of meeting the problem. Finally, large packets containing useful materials were shipped off to Alaska.

The political purges in the Soviet Union in 1936 and 1937 and 1938 touched off all sorts of fireworks at T.C. Many of the students who had been influenced by the social democratic philosophy of men like George Counts, John Childs, and William Kilpatrick regarded the trials as confirmation of Stalinist absolutism. In turn, they were denounced as Trotskyites and fascist diversionaries by the extreme left.

Every new thrust of Adolf Hitler produced deepening concern at T.C. Neither faculty nor students had to wait for the absorption of Czechoslovakia to know what was happening. The first appearance of *Mein Kampf* in American editions was enough to produce boiling classroom discussions.

I think I may have said enough to indicate that T.C. in the mid-thirties was a forcing-house of intellectual and political activity. Classrooms were more than a site for instruction; they were arenas for ideological combat. No one felt deprived; all had a wide range of options if they hungered for controversy. T.C. as a whole not infrequently was at odds with the administrative decisions of Nicholas Murray Butler, president of Columbia University. Nor was there any paucity of differences between some members of the faculty and Dean William Russell. Within the faculty itself were fascinating ideological and philosophical divisions. William Kilpatrick and William Bagley were frequently juxtaposed. George Counts and Roma Gans, if I remember correctly, had some interesting exchanges. And the students vibrated from one issue to the next.

T.C. was more than a graduate school at Columbia; it set the intellectual and philosophical tone for the University and, indeed, for a large segment of the national liberal community. Just by sheer candlepower T.C. lit up a substantial part of the United States educational firmament. Perhaps most important of all, T.C. helped to define the nature of academic and intellectual freedom at a critical time in American history. Men like Kilpatrick, Counts, Rugg, Watson, Childs, Nelon, Norton, and Miller could be counted upon to produce a climate of free inquiry just in the act of serving on the same faculty. The ideas that came to life in their courses were not confined to the theoretical; they generated electrical power for change throughout the nation.

Thirty years later, personal memories are still strong. I recall, for example, visits of celebrities to Clyde Miller's course on propaganda analysis. One of the visitors was James J. Walker, only a few years out of the New York City mayoralty. Walker circled the high desk at the front of the big lecture room. "If I seem to be looking for something," he said, "it's only a bar on which to raise my foot." After the laughter subsided, he said he supposed the reason Professor Miller had invited him to the class was to tell the students something about politics.

"I can tell you everything I know about politics in just six words. *Pick the man who can win,*" he said. "This answers most of the questions on politics. How do you choose from among a large number of candidates? How do you decide whether you ought to go into politics? How do you determine whether any given officeholder should run for re-election? Am I being cynical? I don't think so. The man who can win gets there because people like him. And he knows the best way to keep people liking him is to give them something to like. The biggest vote-getters don't always make the best officeholders but, by and large, they hold up pretty well."

One of the students asked Walker whether he felt any resentment toward F.D.R. for having ousted him, thus converting him, in effect, into a stepping stone to the Presidency. Walker smiled. "This brings me to the second thing I learned in politics," he said. "No grudges."

Another visitor who made a strong impression on the students was George Gallup. Political polling was still an early art in those days. Gallup spoke of the long-term possibilities of polling, but also warned that unscientific techniques could produce mammoth errors. Some years later, after the Truman-Dewey contest of 1948, I had occasion to reflect on this statement.

Other memories of T.C. in the mid-thirties: Harold Rugg surrounded by the inevitable cluster of students at the end of a lecture, then looking up and saying, "Good heavens, I was supposed to be at a faculty conference a half hour ago!" . . . A visit to John Dewey at his home, talking about his view of the Trotsky assassination and about the Soviet purges . . .

William Kilpatrick talking about the need to educate for world citizenship . . . Goodwin Watson defending the right of the artist to experiment with new forms . . . Ben Fine sitting in his tiny press-relations office near the main entrance and counting columns of newspaper notice for T.C. His competence in the field won him before long the top job in educational journalism in the U.S., education editor of the New York *Times* . . . Violet Edwards of the T.C. administrative staff, who was later to be my chief administrative officer on the Connecticut Education Fact-Finding Commission.

Of all the distinctions and achievements of T.C. in those days, the one that may have had the greatest historical impact is the basic philosophical development of the non-Communist left in the United States. At a time when many intellectuals were giving up on American political and economic institutions and turning to the Soviet Union, the key figures of T.C. —Counts, Kilpatrick, Rugg, Childs, et al.—with the full backing of John Dewey, were redefining the nature and place of vital progressive social-democratic thought and action. In many ways, they were the custodians of the American liberal tradition given spirit and substance by Jefferson, Emerson, William James, and Oliver Wendell Holmes. Their advocacy came at a time when the democratic process was undergoing its greatest strain. They helped provide for American students and intellectuals an approach to social planning that refuted the monopoly claims of the left extremists. They examined Marx without illusion, prejudice, or preconception. They provided that most valuable of all possessions in a free society— genuine options. They demonstrated that it was not necessary to look at the Soviet Union uncritically in order to maintain intellectual respectability. They believed in testing their propositions and in comprehending those aspects of the American tradition that made change possible.

As I say, of all the solid contributions of T.C. to the world of education or American intellectual development, none stands higher than the part it played in the enlargement of twentieth-century American progressivism. Education, as Dewey said, is a matter of doing. And T.C. did.

The *Jester*
and the *Times*

≽⋇≾⊹≽⋇≾

by *Corey Ford*

I had secured a position as Columbia correspondent with the New York *Times* to help pay my expenses at college, but I'm afraid the *Times* did not get its $12-a-week's worth. I was far too busy writing on my own. In addition to running the *Jester*, I had appointed myself its drama critic, an enviable position, since I received free review tickets to all the Broadway plays. Thus it became my critical lot to pass judgment on the annual Columbia Varsity Show, written and composed by three classmates of mine. I panned it unmercifully and, with rare critical foresight, predicted that its creators would never

---

COREY FORD, *in the College from 1919 to 1923, most recently reminisced about people and places of the 1920s in* A Time of Laughter (*Little, Brown*), *as part of which this essay was written.*

be heard from again. The book was by Oscar Hammerstein II, the lyrics by Lorenz Hart, and the musical score by Richard Rodgers.

I had bragged rashly in my review that I could do a better job myself, and accordingly I was challenged to write the book and lyrics of the 1923 Varsity Show. *Half Moon Inn,* with music by Ray Webb and Morris Watkins, played a week at the Astor Hotel on Broadway, and the downtown critics were far kinder than I had been to its predecessor. At about that time, the Alumni Federation was offering a prize for a Columbia football song, so I concocted new words for the final chorus of the show and sent the entry in. The whole thing slipped my mind until the telephone at the fraternity house rang one midnight, and the irate editor of the *Times* roared, "I thought you were supposed to be our Columbia correspondent. We've just had a dispatch giving the results of their Alumni Federation song contest." I told him I hadn't heard anything about it. "Well, go out and interview the winner. His name is . . ." A slight pause. "Goddamnit, it's you." And that was how I learned that "Roar, Lion, Roar" had won the prize.

If I was neglecting my duties with the *Times,* I displayed an even greater disregard for my studies. I was taking a course in eighteenth-century literature with Professor Harrison Ross Steeves; but I was so involved with extracurricular activities that I failed to crack a book and had to skip the examination. Professor Steeves kindly arranged for me to take an oral test in his office a week later, but once again I was too busy to do any reading and arrived at his office totally unprepared but resolved to bluff it through somehow. Professor

Steeves was tall and saturnine—he reminded me of the pictures of Sherlock Holmes—with a keen sense of humor, which showed in his veiled blue eyes and quizzical half smile. When he asked me the first question about Smollett's *Peregrine Pickle,* and I identified the leading character as female, he ended his examination abruptly and leaned back and regarded me for a thoughtful moment. "Mr. Ford," he said, "it is quite obvious that you are not interested in eighteenth-century writers. Perhaps this would interest you more." He took a book from the shelf behind him and handed it to me. "Have you ever read Max Beerbohm's *A Christmas Garland?* Take it home with you. We'll call it C for the course." That was my introduction to Beerbohm's parodies; and I think Professor Steeve's amused understanding had as much as anything to do with my becoming a literary satirist.

I had another professor at Columbia who was less understanding, but who had his inadvertent share in furthering my career. I had signed up for a senior course in creative writing with John Erskine, a pompous Tennysonian figure who seemed to me totally devoid of humor, and who read aloud the compositions of the class in a sonorous voice, which usually put me to sleep. The composition chosen for one session was a long and dreary account of slum life, full of mildewed walls and clogged plumbing and rats; but Erskine praised it as a work of great art and insisted on reading every last word to us. For my own composition the following week, I submitted a parody of this work of great art, which annoyed Erskine so much that he gave me a flat F and called it "an example of undergraduate impertinence." I mentioned the incident to Professor Steeves, and he suggested, with that familiar small smile, "Why don't you submit it to *Life?*" It was my first published article, and I had the satisfaction of waving the check under Erskine's nose. On the other hand, he had the satisfaction of flunking me in the course.

A Doubled Magic

⋟⋇⊹⊹⋟⋇

by Herman Wouk

Any husband is forgiven for believing his wife is the finest woman in the world; and any alumnus will probably be forgiven for thinking his alma mater is the best college in the world.

Few of us Columbians would maintain in cold blood, in an open discussion, that there is no better school anywhere.

HERMAN WOUK, *1934 College and* Jester, *wrote radio comedy for Fred Allen, gathered four campaign stars and a unit citation as a naval officer in World War II, and won a Pulitzer Prize for* The Caine Mutiny, *which became Broadway's* The Caine Mutiny Court Martial *a year later. A version of this essay was delivered during the presentation in 1956 of the Alexander Hamilton Award to Richard Rodgers and Oscar Hammerstein II.*

86   UNIVERSITY ON THE HEIGHTS

We have more pressing matters to argue about. But in our hearts most of us hold, I am sure, a sense of great privilege in having spent our college years on Morningside Heights. We can hardly believe that we could have made a happier choice.

Now why is this so?

Some schools have considerable social chic, and a special few have something like intellectual chic: Columbia is a distinguished school, but I would not call it chic. Some have campuses of rare beauty: the campus of Columbia is pleasant, but not beautiful. Some schools have massively successful football teams: Columbia's teams do not answer to this description. Some schools are placed in spacious towns, full of quiet charming homes and soft green lawns; Columbia is cramped in the middle of a small island full of craggy buildings, wild noise, and insane running-about.

What, then, is there to love about Columbia?

The first course I attended at Columbia—the first day, the first hour of my freshman year—was called Contemporary Civilization. At the time this name was just a label, a label that soon came to have unpleasant connotations of long assignments and heavy going. No doubt the name, if it is still used, has the same connotations today for the freshmen of the class of 1970 (the class of 1970, boys . . . God help us all). But we are far from our freshman days. And all of us, more or less, are living still on the transfusion that Columbia gave us of Contemporary Civilization.

For the secret of Columbia, I suggest, is that it is so uniquely saturated with the sounds and the sights, the rhythms and the values, of civilization as it actually exists today.

Within the rectilinear boundaries of 114th Street and 120th Street, of Broadway and Morningside Drive, there is a peaceful oasis—I had almost said a hallowed oasis—of the life of the mind, defiantly independent of the surrounding market-place racket of Manhattan. There is quiet here, and space, and charm, and pleasant green vistas—in the realm of lasting things. Here in this concourse of red-and-gray buildings, Kant is no mere name, Marx no mere bogey, Shakespeare no mere idol to be nodded to and otherwise ignored: and the nucleus of the atom is no mere vague nightmare. At Columbia these things are life itself.

I do not want to overstate the case. When raccoon coats were the fashion, there were raccoon coats at Columbia: and whatever the current collegiate foolishness may be, there is plenty of it on the Van Am Quadrangle, you may be sure. The wonderful thing about Columbia is that there is also the life of the mind at its highest current mark for those who want it—and that so many students do want it.

What makes a good wife precious to a happy husband, I suppose, is that she brings out the best in him, makes him desire to be his best self: while she herself is yet deliciously human, and wants him to be human too. That is what Columbia is like. I do not remember it as an arty or austere or pretentious place. You could be a rattlebrained hip-flask fool if you wished, and sneak through four years with low grades. But you would have to sneak, for that was not a smart or brave pattern at Columbia, but a jejune one. If you dreamed of distinction or achievement you were at the right address. Tasks measured to your capacity, or urging you to enlarge your capacity, were everywhere, in the curriculum or in the extracurricular activities. Men of the first rank in intellectual pursuits were there to challenge and to guide you. The air was alive with discovery, with the vibrations of intelligence.

It was too rich a diet, too fast a pace, for most young men to keep up with all the year long. There was the recurring urge to say the hell with it, and go off for a few beers, or better yet to find a girl and go out somewhere. And that was when Columbia shone. For at hand, as a quick change from the world of timeless values and hard intellectual work, was the wonderland of cynical, sophisticated, up-to-the-second New York. You could plunge in half an hour from Thorstein Veblen to Ethel Merman, from integral calculus to Jascha Heifetz or Louis Armstrong. The limits were solely economic: a college boy's purse is usually lean. But who of us does not remember balcony seats with a lovely girl at a hypnotic play or concert? You could have your beer in Greenwich Village for very little money, if you wished, and see sights and hear talk that were a second education. If you and your girl liked art, you could go and look at the finest paintings in the new world. The best things of the moment were outside the rectangle of Columbia: the best things of all human history and thought were inside the rectangle. If only you had the sense, you could spend four years in an unforgettably exciting and improving alternation between two realms of magic.

I did. That doubled magic is lasting me a lifetime. All my writings, such as they are, trace back in one sense or another to my four years at Columbia.

As We Were

༈༺✦✧✦༻༈

by Jacques Barzun

Some years ago, while traveling in Nova Scotia, I stopped off
at the Dalhousie University, in Halifax, to visit King's College,
which had been for some time a part of the younger and
larger institution. It was summer and the place was deserted,
except for an elderly scholar who courteously showed me
around. In the course of our tour I said I came from Columbia
and rashly added that I thereby felt able to claim equal descent with him from the original King's College.

At this his humorous eye took on a hard glitter and his

JACQUES BARZUN, *1927 College, 1928 M.A., 1932 Ph.D.*,
has taught history on Morningside for more than forty years,
while filling in the interstices as dean of graduate faculties,
dean of faculties and provost, author, editor, and critic. He
is now University Professor at Columbia.

clear voice an acid note: "Descent! Descent!" said he, "to be sure—illegitimate!" And half serious, half joking, he went on to reproach me personally for holding on to King George's charter and the symbol of the crown. The charge was dishonesty compounded with bad logic. "What has a crown to do with a place called Columbia? Your proper symbol is a pigeon!" Perhaps it was my catching his Latin play on words that mollified him. We chatted pleasantly of other things, but on parting he treated himself to another dig: "You may think you're properly attached to your dubious past, but tradition, loyalty, you can't have any idea of. Loyalty went out of you in 1775."

He said 1775 and I did not argue. Nor did I go on to tell him what was passing through my mind about dates and tradition and loyalty. I might have reminded him that his legitimate and traditional college had not always been on its present campus, and that following a break of fifteen years after the Revolution it had vegetated at Windsor, N.S., until 1923—which happened to be the year I entered Columbia College. Such thoughts naturally led me to recall my college as it was in 1923 and to ask myself about tradition, loyalty, and the rest. What were the feelings of the youth of that time, now well past middle age?

It was certainly not antiquity or continuity that worked on our minds and spirits. Many of the buildings had come into existence later than ourselves and we did not rightly value their spaciousness. "The College at Forty-ninth Street" was a phrase familiar enough, but it raised no picture except the false one of speakeasies in brownstone fronts. And the words roused no feelings except those we might borrow from the witty reminiscences of the eloquent William Barclay Parsons, chairman of the Trustees. To us, again, Van Am was a quadrangle and not a man. We felt much more reverence for Dean Hawkes, visible through the wide-open door of 208 Hamilton, and much more affection for Blue Pete, the cyanotic guard who patrolled South Field in company with a decrepit and irreplaceable gray mare.

In short, we were intensely attached to the present, and this for a reason which was peculiar to the times. The mid-1920s in the College were extraordinary years for boys of seventeen, because of the men of twenty-two to twenty-five recently returned from the European war. These elders were not only mature chronologically, they were tempered by the experience of evil. Some were bitter, others cynical and gay, many were highly gifted; they led everything in the College without even trying; and although only a few foolish kids hoped to imitate them, all the rest who had any sensitivity picked up, without effort, from the atmosphere, attitudes and ideas very different from those rightly despised as collegiate. Whether it was the tone and style of *Spectator* and the other publications, or the solidity and breadth of class discussions, or the intermittent friendships that bridged the unusual gap between senior and sophomore, at every turn that special influence made for ripening.

These ex-soldiers were almost all characters. Not yet accustomed to being nursed by a welfare state, or bid for by a highly professionalized world reeking of culture, these men came back to the College of their own motion, having developed their own tastes. If they asserted the value of brains or of literature it was not from conformity with a trend, but in opposition to the many whose hope and goal was to be bond salesmen and to own a Stutz roadster as soon as possible. There was still in those days plenty of philistinism and business complacency to bang one's head against to see if it was soft. And the Establishment had not yet learned the disabling ploy of bland self-reproach and moral masochism.

One result for us of that real battle was the presence of enthusiasm—sometimes cheerful, sometimes angry, sometimes routed by despair, but stubborn enough to make demands on life. And these demands were encouraged, as the whole undergraduate enterprise was encouraged, by the men who taught us. The younger among them had also been in the war; the political scientists and historians had taken part as junior aides in the Peace Conference. The latest comers to academic life had by struggle managed to establish the Contemporary Civilization course. Erskine, picking up a hint of Woodberry's, had initiated the Great Books as an honors program. The mood of reconstruction after the catastrophe of 1914–18 was contagious and civilizing. It is no wonder that our attachment was to the living present. We did not use loathsome words like *prestige* and *image* to rake up old glories, for colleges then did not know they were supposed to advertise and compete. The best part of tradition, we thought in our brashness, was addition. T. S. Eliot confirmed our belief, and what was going on around us that we gave our hearts to was the work of hands and minds active now, not of machinery and plan spinners for a specious future.

All this I could have told my peppery host at King's College and perhaps persuaded him that colleges and tradition and loyalty are creatures of chance like other things. Charters and crowns are useful reminders of what has been and what can be, but they have no generative virtue in themselves. Nor can deeds be had to order. They require a happy conjunction of men and circumstance, after which attachment and gratitude are natural and easy.

The Woodberry Years

ᵉᵏᵗᵗᵗᵗᵏᵉ

by Melville Cane

My first personal meeting with George Edward Woodberry
was in the middle of my sophomore year. I was standing in
the corridor before his lecture hour when he came out of his
office, in Fayerweather Hall, notes and reference books in
hand. To my astonishment he stopped in front of me and
without warning asked whether I'd take dinner with him that
night. I was so overcome that all I could muster up was
a transparent falsehood. I pleaded a previous engagement.

MELVILLE CANE, *1900 College, 1903 Law, has been a
lawyer, a poet, and a dedicated alumnus for just about as long
as the twentieth century has been raging its course through
history. His contribution is edited from an address at the
University convocation in honor of George Edward Woodberry in 1948.*

Woodberry merely smiled, expressed regret, and walked on.

A few days later, however, he greeted me again. "I wonder," he inquired soberly, "whether you expect to be hungry a week from tonight?" I assured him I so expected. That was the introduction to our friendship.

If I adopt a less than solemn tone it is because of the circumstances. This memorial, unlike most, is removed from the atmosphere of death by an interval of many years; it takes us back, in fact, half a century, when Erskine and I were undergraduates, when the world was fresh and young, and Woodberry was our god.

Distinguished alike as poet, biographer, and literary essayist, especially noted as an editor of Shelley and a biographer of Poe and Hawthorne, he will always be cherished by those who sat in his classes rather as a great teacher, a great spirit. In the truest and finest sense he was the friend and guide of youth. His teaching years, though not continuous, covered over one half of his total span. Not long after his graduation from Harvard in 1877 he was called to the University of Nebraska. A quarter of a century later he was lecturing in institutions as far apart as our eastern and western coasts; Amherst, Stanford, Wisconsin, Cornell, Kenyon, all claimed him for a semester or special course. But it was his twelve years at Columbia that were richest and most concentrated in influence, and, I think, his happiest, most rewarding period.

In 1891 Columbia was still a small local college, confined within a city block. Seth Low had just been made its president. It was Mr. Low's desire and design to create a great university, great not so much in buildings as in the quality of its faculty. In his search he turned for guidance to Charles

Eliot Norton and James Russell Lowell. On their recommendation, he appointed Woodberry to a chair in literature.

It is of course next to impossible to communicate, now, the mystery of his charm. Other fine teachers have given courses in English literature and in the history and theory of literary criticism, but who could compare with him? We like to believe he had no equal. As supporting testimony I give you the impressions of two men, usually cautious in praise, the scientist, Hans Zinsser, and the editor of the *Atlantic*, Ferris Greenslet. Zinsser in his autobiography affirms: "He was unquestionably one of the greatest teachers this country has ever seen, inspiring with his own passionate sincerity a large and diverse group of young men, few of whom, whatever their subsequent occupations, ever lost entirely the imprint of his personality."

And Greenslet writes: "His letters contained certain references to 'the illusion about me.' Yet every word of his characterization of the followers of his master Shelley is literally true of his own: 'This sentiment of direct, intimate, intense personal loyalty which he has inspired in them is rare if not unparalleled in literary annals.' "

He was never a seeker after recognition or reputation. Shy, reticent, hampered somewhat by defective eyesight, his tendency was to withdraw rather than to make advances. And yet with each succeeding year his classes grew and he was elected the favorite professor.

It was a heterogeneous mass of undergraduates, not remarkable for literacy, in many cases with athletics as their major interest. They came and urged still others to come, and not because they were snap courses. They weren't. But they happened to be given by a man more concerned with the spirit than the letter, who dealt with universals under the aspect of eternity, who converted the unseen into eloquent, vivid reality.

Boys, even the most unawakened, unconsciously grow aware. These Columbia boys sensed his essential humanity, his power of evoking an ideal world. Through his lack of professorial formality they were encouraged to share his cultural wealth. Perhaps for the first time in their lives they understood the deep meaning of the phrase "a gentleman and a scholar."

He was not unsociable, as some mistakenly have charged. He had the heart of a democrat but the selectiveness of an aristocrat. Fortunate, indeed, was that boy who was invited down to 5 East Seventeenth Street for an evening of talk before the log fire in the friendly room. Talk of travel in strange lands—Italy, Greece, Sicily. Mock-serious pronouncements on the relative virtues of martinis and manhattans. Tales of the realms of gold, recorded by poets through the ages. Talk running deep into the night as the air grew bluer with the smoke of his cigar—it was always a Rosa de Paris— as the logs in the grate sagged to embers.

Or again, on some other night, dinner at the Everett House, or Logerot's on lower Fifth Avenue, or The Century, or The Players, or, on some high occasion, at the old Delmonico's. Thereafter, perhaps, an experiment with Aristotelian pity and terror in the guise of *The King of the Opium Ring* at the Academy of Music on Irving Place.

One day in 1898 the *Columbia Spectator* printed a letter written by an undergraduate to his parents, and released by them after the boy's death. It is a report of his visit to Woodberry to discuss a graduation thesis.

"I sum up the whole of our conversation in one phrase, 'ideal living'—and we touched—or at least he did (for I was spellbound), we touched upon numerous territories of thought and learning. To express it more clearly, perhaps I would call it a dissertation on culture, not of mind and intellect alone (which he claims is only half), but of the heart, a general culture as it were, so intimately associated with every word or act of life that it becomes life itself.

"Everything else that has occurred this week palls so utterly in comparison . . . that I hardly think it worth while noting."

The Woodberry years at Columbia constituted a truly Augustan age of letters. He gave student writing a fresh impulse. The moribund *Columbia Literary Monthly* took on new life. A more sprightly, pert rival, *The Morningside,* was born and thrived. Among contributors and editors were Springarn, Keppel, the Alsbergs (Carl and Henry), Alfred Kroeber, Zinsser, Louis Ledoux, Strunsky, Alfred Cohn, and Henry Sydnor Harrison.

James Rosenberg and Joseph Proskauer edited an anthology of Columbia verse. Later, after graduation, Will Bradley and George Hellman founded a new literary magazine, *East and West;* in it appeared the first canto of Woodberry's philosophic poem "The Roamer." Bradley and Harold Kellock also collaborated on a collection of "Imaginary Lectures," gay and impudent takeoffs on the faculty. The one Woodberry enjoyed most was the parody of himself. The subject on the fancied occasion was "Mother Goose's Melodies." During its delivery the lecturer would pause from time to time, characteristically stumped in the middle of a quotation, stopping "to give his favorite Mona Lisa smile."

Perhaps as great a service as any was the formation, under Woodberry's incentive, of Kings Crown as an undergraduate literary and social club open to all comers. Meetings were held in the College Tavern, a questionable shack, perched on an unblasted rock, and now superseded by the Union Theological Seminary. Here, over beer and sandwiches, fledglings would read their latest poems and stories, to be addressed on occasion by contemporary celebrities—Edmund Clarence Stedman, Harry Thurston Peck, Dr. S. Weir Mitchell, Colonel Higginson, John La Farge, and others.

On the graduate side Woodberry became the first editor of *The Journal of Comparative Literature* and established a series of studies in the same field, the fruits of the research of younger scholars such as Springarn, John Garrett Underhill, Frank Wadleigh Chandler, John Smith Harrison, Lewis Einstein, Lewis N. Chase, and Henry Osborn Taylor.

In quite a different role Woodberry served as faculty adviser of athletics when football was revived at the turn of the century. In a moving poem dedicated to the Class of 1903, the last he taught at Columbia, he not only pays warm tribute to the prowess of halfback Harold Weekes, but rejoices in his own participation in student life:

A thousand times the loud Columbia cheer,
Linked with my name, has fallen upon my ear,
Sweeter and sweeter with each passing year.

Though yours the last with those of old combine,
A thousand young Columbia hearts are mine,
Though yours the last, crowning the happy line.

The influence of Woodberry soon spread beyond the campus to alumni life; more than any other individual he was responsible for the successful formation of the Columbia University Club. Later a group of his former students, with other admirers, in turn founded a club in his honor, The Woodberry Society, which published many of his later poems and essays.

Its first meeting, held at the Grolier Club on November 29, 1911, was a distinguished occasion. Woodberry came down from his ancestral home in Beverly, Massachusetts, to deliver an address on Wendell Phillips, the great abolitionist. His appearance was quite in contrast to the slightly rumpled, home-spun figure we had been accustomed to confront in class, for now he was most carefully and formally attired in white tie and tails. Phillips was his boyhood hero; he had known him, face to face, on the streets of the town in Civil War days, and his tribute reflected depths of feeling born of childhood memories.

The Phillips address is probably the fullest expression of Woodberry's Americanism and of his conception of the role of the scholar in the Republic. The following extracts disclose both his position as citizen as well as his faith in the democratic process:

"Civilization laughs at institutions. Order, in the sense of fixity and permanence of what is, which society enjoins and old men love, is a defective conception of public well-being. It may be heaven's first law, but heaven is a finished place. Change is the password of growing states. . . .

"America's title to glory among the nations is her service to human liberty. I can bear that we should fail, relatively, in art and letters, have little sense of beauty, or skill in man's highest wisdom, philosophic thought, or in his highest faculty, imagination, but I cannot bear that we should fail in justice.

. . . Death is not the worst of life. Defeat is not the worst of failures. Not to have tried is the true failure."

As I have endeavored to indicate earlier, it was the man that counted first with his students; literature, his especial subject, held the greater values in consequence.

John Erskine's tribute in our senior yearbook, *The Naughty-Naughtian,* is both apt and accurate:

> One who took manhood for his art,
> Taught it by manliness so rare
> We keep his lessons in our heart,
> But first of all he entered there.

The cardinal tenet in Woodberry's creed was that literature was worth studying and producing only as an enrichment of life. Through the Columbia years he constantly reformulated his position. In final shape it crystallized in his essay "A New Defense of Poetry," published in 1899 in the volume entitled *Heart of Man,* but used long before in his criticism course. This "defense" belongs of right to the noble line of Sidney and Shelley.

Who will ever forget the sound of the voice, low, deliberate, musical; the fervor, with difficulty controlled, as he read from the proof sheets:

"Man only is of prime interest to man; and man as a spirit, a creature but made in the likeness of something divine. . . . Conscience and imagination were the pioneers who made earth habitable for the human spirit; they are still its lawgivers; and where they have lodged their treasures, there is wisdom."

And who will ever fail to feel the electricity with which

that classroom in Fayerweather Hall was charged, as he summed up:

"What then is the ideal life? It is to make one's life a poem, as Milton dreamed of the true poet; for as art works through matter and takes on concrete and sensible shape with its mortal conditions, so the soul dips in life, is in material action, and suffering a similar fate sinks into limitations and externals of this world and this flesh. In such a life, mortal in all ways, to bring down the vision that floats in the soul's eyes, the ideal order as it is revealed to the poet's gaze, incorporating it in deed and being, and to make it prevail, so far as our lives have power, in the world of our life, is the task set for us. . . .

"It is a message blended of many voices of the poets whom Shelley called, whatever might be their calamity on earth, the most fortunate of men; it rises from all lands, all ages, all religions; it is the battle cry of that one idea whose slow and hesitating growth is the unfolding of our long civilization, seeking to realize in democracy the earthly, and in Christianity the heavenly, hope of man—the idea of the community of the soul, the sameness of it in all men. To lead this life is to be one with man through love, one with the universe through knowledge, one with God through the will; that is its goal, toward that we strive, in that we believe."

I hope I have suggested some impression of the man whose example and whose words have nourished and sustained so many of us through the advancing years.

Francis J. Ryan

ᕼᔑᐧᐧᔑᕼ

by Joshua Lederberg

A great university is measured by the caliber of the men it can attract and maintain in a free community of scholars. In my own scientific career, one great man was a pre-eminent formative influence—Francis J. Ryan, professor of Zoology at Columbia University. Ryan was a Columbia man throughout: A.B. (1937), Ph.D. (1941), and then a professor until a sudden fatal heart attack in 1963 at the age of forty-seven.

I first met Ryan when I was a Columbia College sophomore in 1942. He had just returned from a year's postdoctoral re-

JOSHUA LEDERBERG, *1944 College, student at Columbia College of Physicians and Surgeons from 1944 to 1946, and Ph.D. from Yale in 1947, was a Nobel laureate in 1958 in physiology and medicine for research in genetics of bacteria. He is now at Stanford.*

search fellowship at Stanford. He had intended to work on embryological physiology in frogs, but there he met G. W. Beadle and E. L. Tatum, who were rapidly pushing ahead after their first epochal findings in the biochemical genetics of Neurospora. He was perhaps foolhardy to bring this botanical material—the red bread mold—back to a department of Zoology, but he was too good a biologist to be deterred by niceties like plant versus animal in deciding how to study fundamental issues of life. Besides, this mold grew so quickly that it would put up a good race with a lame snail. So one could pretend to imbue it with the animal virtue of locomotion.

The excitement of a biochemical approach to genetics was infectious, and I soon begged him for a chance to learn the tricks of this new game. He arranged a laboratory job for me, glassware washing at first; later, technical work in microbiology, that not only helped me through that year of college, but taught me much of the discipline of laboratory research. Above all, it gave me the opportunity to sharpen my adolescent thinking against one of the most versatile, most generous minds I would ever encounter. In retrospect, I can perceive more clearly what a unique quality he had for focusing on his students' development even at the expense of a professorial ego. He rarely instructed me about anything, but would often lead me into an intellectual trap, then challenge me to find my own way out of it.

In 1944, Avery, McCarty, and MacLeod of the Rockefeller Institute published their historic paper on the identification of DNA as the "transforming factor" in certain bacteria. This work aroused great interest as a strong indication that the gene was composed of DNA. It was not yet conclusive for it was still controversial whether bacteria could even be thought of as having a genetics. The details of this bacterial "transforming factor" still left very reasonable questions about its analogy to the genes of higher organisms with well-defined chromosomes, like Neurospora, fruit flies, or man. In a bull session, Ryan and I soon agreed that it would be exciting to try experiments on the possibility of a similar transforming effect of DNA in Neurospora.

The advantage of Neurospora was that, on the one hand, it could be easily manipulated as laboratory material for microbial genetics. Experiments that would take years with mice, and months with fruit flies, could be done in a few days. Furthermore, one could perform biochemical tests with billions of individual cell nuclei in a small flask. On the other hand, Neurospora could be cross-bred (unlike, as we then thought, other simpler microbes) and apparent genetic changes subjected to thorough analysis by test crosses, in close analogy to the genetics of other well-studied organisms.

The experimental design was impeccable—but it never worked. In fact, to this day we have no very clear example of the incorporation of purified DNA molecules into existing chromosomes of cells of higher forms. If we failed to achieve our original aims, however, there were several useful by-products. For one thing, we discovered the occasional occurrence of spontaneous reversions of a mutant gene back to the original normal type, and it was an occasion of great pride to co-author this with Ryan as my debut in scientific publication. Far more important, this work laid the methodological groundwork for systematic searches for rare genetic events occurring in large cell populations.

One day I suggested that we ring the changes on our experimental approach. Instead of trying to make Neurospora imitate a phenomenon recently worked out in bacteria, we could use similar methods to inquire whether bacteria had genetic mechanisms similar to Neurospora.

Ryan immediately perceived the potentialities of this approach, and thereafter spared no effort to create the opportunity for me to explore them. We did start some experiments on bacterial recombination at Columbia, but they were inconclusive. (Later we were to know that the particular strains of bacteria we used then were inappropriate, but there could have been no way to tell this beforehand.)

By this time, I had begun my training at Columbia Medical School, while continuing part-time research with Ryan at Morningside Heights. By a fortunate coincidence, the midquarter of the junior year was allocated to elective work, and Ed Tatum had just then taken a chair at Yale University. During 1945, Ryan had learned that Tatum had already initiated some similar steps toward a bacterial genetics, having already published a brief note on biochemical mutants of *Escherichia coli* in 1944. Ryan suggested that I ask Tatum to sponsor me as a research fellow at Yale to pursue this work —and of course must have recommended me to him, for I was promptly accepted.

When I met Tatum, I found he had already been thinking along similar lines for some time, but his active work on the problem had been disrupted by moving and the reorganization of a new laboratory. I arrived in New Haven in March 1946, just when he was restarting his own work. This is not the place to recount that happy story; briefly, the fellowship lengthened into a year's leave, and eventually into a dropout from Columbia Medical School. My research with Tatum went too well to be interrupted, and Columbia courses were readily accepted for credit toward a Yale Ph.D. In fact, I was officially registered for elective work (off campus) in the Columbia M.D. program while doing the research that became my Yale Ph.D. dissertation in 1947. Fortunately, these technicalities were overlooked at the time.

To my regret, I had only occasional visits with Ryan after that, but they were always a lift to the spirit and a challenge to the mind.

In 1958, I was somewhat bewildered to find myself in Stockholm on a platform with Beadle and Tatum, to share a Nobel Prize of which my part was based on these studies on genetic recombination in bacteria. Perhaps only a knowledgeable circle knew, as we did, of Ryan's part in them. Any such awards are bound to be arbitrary, and a thoughtful observer will always look for the teacher behind the student.

In many ways Ryan was ahead of his time; but he also insisted on keeping a firm hold on traditional biology as well as its innovations in biochemistry and microbiology. He was also keenly alert to the human uses and misuses of scientific knowledge: for him, biology was one of the essential humanities. Some of his insights into modern biology were too advanced to get the priority they deserved, even taking account of the pressure of legitimate but conflicting demands on the resources of a great university. The winds of change are blowing again, and he might now look forward with greater confidence that the university he loved so well would regain its historic pre-eminence in research and teaching about the fundamentals of life.

The Extracurricular Grind

꙼❖꙼

by Richard Rodgers

No one ever displayed more hunger for Columbia than I. It began before I went to Morningside Heights, when I was a student at De Witt Clinton High. I didn't like Clinton at all and I kept remembering that Columbia produced the best musical shows of any college. I simply had to get there, and fast. It was simple enough. I just enrolled at summer session and took the courses I needed to complete my last year of high school. The French teacher at summer school was a real live Frenchman and the English prof came fresh from Oxford. They fired my passion for knowledge to such an extent

RICHARD RODGERS *never made it to graduation in 1923, but was awarded the Mus.D. in 1954.* South Pacific, Oklahoma, The King and I *are a small and precious sample of the glittering treasury of musical comedies that are his.*

that I could hardly wait for the fall term to begin so that I could start work on a Varsity Show. The score that Larry Hart and I wrote had to be submitted in a breathtaking competition before a three-man committee composed of Ray Perkins, Dick Conreid, and Oscar Hammerstein II. There was only one other contesting show. We won.

Having had my first taste of higher education my appetite was insatiable. I attended Varsity Show auditions. I wrote and rewrote with Larry. I played piano for long rehearsals that spanned a period of months. These practice sessions took place in the basement of one of the larger halls of knowledge on campus. Some of this knowledge had to seep down to me, didn't it? There was so much for an eager student to learn: never turn your back on the audience in singing a song; don't drop your voice at the end of a sentence; pace is not achieved by speed alone.

By the time we moved into the Hotel Astor ballroom for dress rehearsals perhaps I knew less about calculus than some of my friends, but certainly I knew more about lyric projection and the technique of getting a laugh without a funny line.

Besides Larry Hart, seven years my senior, my most valuable mentor was Roy Webb, who orchestrated my music for the show. He knew very little early English history but he gave me the rudiments of musical notation so that I could make my own piano manuscripts. He also taught me to conduct and I led the professional orchestra at the Astor through all the show's performances. I studied and learned a dependable beat and the delicate art of balance.

My pursuit of academic knowledge was so successful that I decided to plug away at my studies for another year and write a second Varsity Show. The faithfulness of my class attendance earned me the right to the title of Columbia's Number One Drop-In. At the end of my second year of application I came to the conclusion that Columbia had given me all she had to offer. The Institute of Musical Art, now Juilliard, was only a few blocks away and there I went for three enriching and enlightening years.

Rewarding as it was, I shall never cease to be grateful for my Columbia education. No other institution of learning could have offered me, at the age of seventeen, a full course in musical comedy from writing, through selling the stuff, to the exquisite refinement of causing the orchestra to sound its last loud chord at the exact second of impact between the stage floor and the final curtain.

The fruits of knowledge are sweet.

The Golden Day

ᘏᕼᚷᕼᘏ

by M. Halsey Thomas

On the day of the Columbia Bicentennial, having an hour or so to myself, I did some meditating on the two centuries of the institution. It was easy for me to visualize the attractive and tiny Tory-Anglican college on the bank of the Hudson with the debonair Cooper teaching his two dozen or so students, and see it split by political ideas, then swept away by revolution, some graduates in exile and distress, others contributing importantly to the establishment of the new nation. Next came the small and select day school for New Yorkers that continued well through the nineteenth century:

M. HALSEY THOMAS, *1930 B.S., 1931 B.L.S., 1942 M.A., was for more than two decades curator of Columbiana, that remarkable collection about Columbia and its historical context, and is now university archivist at Princeton.*

at the downtown site with Anthon and McVickar dominating
the scene, later in the gaslight and brownstone era of Forty-
ninth Street, where a process of acceleration began, which
has never stopped. The School of Mines under Egleston and
Chandler stirred up the college first, in the years of great
national energy that followed the Civil War; later Burgess
and Butler and the growth of the city turned it into a great
university. The move to Morningside in 1897 was more than
a change of site; it was a coming-of-age.

In my *mythos* I think of the decades between that date and
World War I as the golden day of Columbia. Lloyd Morris,
1914, has told what it was like in his memoirs, *A Threshold
in the Sun:* "At that moment, there existed at Columbia a
constellation of remarkable minds whose effect on the intellectual climate was electric. A student needed only to be
receptive to find his own mind the target of ambient energies.
But he needed to be hardy to support the intensity of their
impact. . . . This tonic, buoyant tone pervaded the American
academic world. [This statement is far too sweeping, and is
an example of what I would call Manhattan myopia. M.H.T.]
But circumstances made it peculiarly inevitable at Columbia.
Among the older American institutions of learning, Columbia
is almost uniquely emancipated from its past. Originally dedicated to the transmission of an official tradition, it seldom
recalls this initial purpose except on commemorative occasions. . . ."

When I first came to Morningside, the scars of the war
years were no longer visible, and much remained from the
golden day, and earlier. Brander Matthews was no longer
driven up to the college behind a pair of fat horses by his

own coachman, but Herbert Livingston Satterlee came to trustee meetings in his 1915 Simplex with liveried chauffeur. A. V. Williams Jackson still wore his cutaway, his purple stock with pearl tiepin, and took off his derby to every acquaintance or student he met. The campus still held many other venerable, dignified figures who had begun their careers at Forty-ninth Street: Charles F. Chandler, the great industrial chemist and public health pioneer, who was just beginning to relax his twenty-hour daily working schedule; Nelson Glenn McCrea, who revealed the Roman world with such interest and charm and assurance that one felt certain he had been there; George C. D. Odell, who had seen every play of importance on the New York stage since the early 1880s, and was compiling his monumental *Annals,* which stood at fifteen volumes at his death. Although he became an international figure, much of the atmosphere of Forty-ninth Street clung to President Butler as long as he lived.

My own teachers belonged to the next generation—the extraordinary faculty assembled by Butler: Franz Boas, pioneer anthropologist, who would lecture for an hour way over our heads, then, after a smoking break, would send in his charming associate, Ruth Benedict, who proceeded to make everything crystal clear; John Dewey, who rarely looked at his class when he lectured, and seemed to be talking to someone upstairs in the next building, but fascinated us by letting us witness his processes of thought as he took an idea, ambled around it, dug up amplifications, disposed of objections, and finally made a statement; William Pepperell Montague, philosopher and superb teacher, who always gave the impression, at his evening lectures, of being comfortably loaded, and discoursed and defended "isms" one after another so brilliantly that we were never able to figure out where he himself stood; Dixon Ryan Fox, historian and generous and kind man of affairs, from whom I learned the virtue of getting things finished and published; Carlton J. H. Hayes, whose tart and dramatic lectures on nationalism, delivered mainly out of the corner of his mouth, seemed in the 1920s to dispose effectively of this unfortunate development, a lesson which has not yet been learned; the austere and godly Evarts Boutell Greene, who not only taught American colonial history but exemplified the integrity of first-class scholarship —which leads me to state my belief that any real and lasting influence that is made on students by a teacher is made by his character rather than his teaching or his subject matter.

I am glad to make public testimony to the excellence of the education which was vouchsafed to me at Columbia. Civilized professors opened up new avenues for me, and interests that have persisted from that day to this; from them I also obtained a decent *Weltanschauung* and sense of values, and the critical background wherewith to reject the phony and the shoddy, which is about all you can ask of a liberal arts education. (Enough of John Dewey rubbed off on me to make me aware that education—and the enlargement of life— is a process that must stop only with rigor mortis.) Another obligation I have is for the job that was done immediately in clearing away the intellectual rubbish that young Americans come to college with; there are very few institutions in which this job is so well done. Anthropology probably did more to educate me than any other subject; philosophy was next. Somehow, being freed from enslavement to ideologies has made it easier to deal adequately with the other great enslavements of men: liquor and women, although this connection may not be immediately obvious. Just being enrolled in a great and respected university in a great city was an education in itself. Here I must quote from Joseph Wood Krutch: "At some time in the course of his experience, every man should rub shoulders with his fellows, experience the excitement of a metropolis' nervous activity; live close to the great, the distinguished, the famous, and the merely notorious—if for no other reason than because only so can he learn properly to discount them, or at least learn in what ways they are, and what ways they are not, to be taken at their own and the world's valuation. . . . Urbanity seems to be literally that: something impossible to acquire except in cities. . . ." (From *The American Scholar*, Spring 1950, XIX, 143).

I do not wish to leave the impression that my student days were entirely devoted to serious matters. I had fun; I obtained considerable education from bull sessions; I tried opera once; I frequently sampled the entertainment offerings of the brothers Minsky (one of them was a Columbia College and Law graduate, so that made it all right); I went to a football game; I drank tea with professors and their wives; I spent weekends at all the Ivy women's colleges except Mount Holyoke; I collected books on Fourth Avenue and on Fifty-ninth Street; I learned that it was easier to get dates with beautiful gals than with plain ones (the beauties were more eager for attention).

I am glad that I was at Columbia in the day of the thirty-five-cent lunch and the dollar dinner, the Broadway trolleys, the open-top double-decker Fifth Avenue buses, the

Nemo Theatre, the Coney Island steamboats, the summer
session dances, the Barnard jungle, star-lit evenings in Riverside Park.

In brief, I am a contented alumnus, and I have no intention of turning in my diplomas and asking for my money back.

An Authentic Past

༃❖⳾╆╆⳾❖༄

by Theodore Caplow

Columbia College in the late thirties was, I am quite sure,
the best undergraduate institution in the United States, but
I had not the slightest inkling of it at the time, nor did most
of my classmates. That a freshman should draw Jacques
Barzun, Herbert Schneider, Mark Van Doren, Joseph Wood
Krutch, and Meyer Schapiro as his teachers and follow them
up with Irwin Edman, Douglas Moore, and Robert Lynd
as a sophomore seemed entirely natural and matter of fact.
It was not until much later, after many years of university
teaching and prolonged exposure to institutions of higher edu-

THEODORE CAPLOW *spent two undergraduate years at the Col-
lege, took his degrees at the University of Chicago, wrote*
The Sociology of Work, *was co-author of* The Academic
Marketplace, *and came back to Columbia to teach.*

cation in the United States and Europe, that I came to appreciate how distinctive the Columbia experience had been.

My stay at Columbia was unusually short, to my present regret. Professor Lynd, with his usual patience and kindness, took my discovery of a sociological vocation seriously, as did Dean Hawkes, who seemed to be continuously aware of everything that happened to his fifteen hundred undergraduates. Columbia's Department of Sociology was thinly staffed; the arrival of Merton and Lazarsfeld and its transformation into the world's leading center of sociological activity was imminent but unforeseen. Lynd agreed that sociology might be studied more advantageously elsewhere; Hawkes gave his blessing and arranged introductions at the University of Chicago; and I left Columbia in the spring of 1938, at the end of my sophomore year, not to return until 1961 when Professor Lynd retired and I took part of his place.

Columbia did not change so very much in the intervening years. The view from the steps of Low Library is not very different now than it was then, although the coal pile that disfigured the southwest corner of the campus has been replaced by Ferris Booth and Carman halls, making a wall around South Field. Even my father remarked recently, looking over the stone balustrade next to Kent, how few visible changes there had been since he attended his last class in 1912. Whether the spiritual landscape has been so immutable is a nice question, and as far as the College is concerned, it is not easily answered by an outside, though nearby, observer. The appearance and attitudes of today's students are markedly different. On the one hand they are more idiosyncratic in dress and manners; on the other, more responsive to social issues and more readily enlisted for collective action. There were students with strong political views then, like Thomas Merton, a man who moved from communism to Catholicism, and the College, then as now, provided freedom of speech as unthinkingly as other utilities. But the world was walled out.

For me the College was not an introduction to practical politics or even to practical social life. I went out for track and the freshman crew, drank beer in late sessions at the Gold Rail, went to dances at Barnard and pursued a raven-haired graduate student who spent her evenings studying aesthetics in the main reading room of South Hall. At one point, I fell in with a circle of primeval hipsters who identified themselves with Columbia without any formal affiliation. Despite these diversions the College seemed to me primarily an intellectual experience; not so much a way of life as the confrontation of raw adolescent minds with an extraordinarily brilliant and unified company of scholars. The unity, I am sure, was largely unconscious, and certainly unintended, but it was so unmistakable that the dozen teachers to whom I was exposed seemed to share a common viewpoint the elements of which have become clearer to me with the passage of time.

To begin with, they had an historical view of the world and one's place in it. In the Midwestern university where I later began to teach, the curriculum was focused on the here-and-now, and American Studies was the most popular undergraduate major. History was viewed backward, so to speak, extending from the American present into an increasingly irrelevant past. At Columbia, history was given as much weight in astronomy and philosophy courses as in the Junior Colloquium. We were perpetually discovering new sets of spiritual ancestors, and were somehow trained to see Athens

and medieval Genoa as solid, real, and no less relevant than
Manhattan. In this sense the College was intensely traditional,
but the symbols that commanded our loyalty were not Columbia's but belonged to something called The Civilization of
the West. The unremitting emphasis on the achievements of
the past often put the present in a poor light, an easy enough
thing to do in the later years of the Great Depression. More
like typical Athenians than typical Americans, we learned to
look back admiringly to the days when giants and heroes
walked the earth, but to look forward with misgivings.

The College's bias in favor of antiquity was accompanied
by a passion for authentication that the whole faculty seemed
to share. We learned that it is always better to read the text
than the commentaries, that excerpts are worthless contrasted
to the full document, that no author can be understood by
reading a single work, that the original language is always
better than a translation and the original edition better than
a modern one with footnotes. Given the choice, most of us
would have preferred manuscripts to printed books and papy-
rus to vellum. This habit of mind forced one into virtuosity
as a reader. Long before rapid-reading schools had been
heard of, Columbia freshmen claimed to reckon their assignments in thousands of pages, and upperclassmen thought
nothing of reading Adam Smith from cover to cover over a
weekend.

The passion for authentication, a virtue of humanists,
generated other norms useful to scientists and social scientists—habits of deferring generalization in favor of particular
facts, of close attention to empirical detail, and of respect for
the diversity and unexpectedness of the real world. There
were certainly a number of grand theorists on the College

faculty, but one never seemed to encounter them in the class-room, where the preference for the particular was overwhelm-ing. It is one of my pleasantest memories that Jacques Barzun's class in the historical background of English litera-ture was permitted to spend several weeks on the single poem that begins "She walks in beauty like the night," our collective curiosity being nearly as inexhaustible as our teacher's pa-tience.

The faculty seemed to have a common inclination to pa-tience. I am still bemused by the recollection of Professor Lynd extracting a notebook from his briefcase and taking care-ful notes on a student's objections to one of his lectures. The Colloquium had two instructors, as it still does. Both listened more than they talked and both read examination papers from beginning to end. The customs of the place were intellectually democratic—one man, one opinion—and I do not ever remember hearing a student silenced by mere authority.

The flaw in this system, if it was a flaw, was that the College did not speak to the total man. It promulgated no model and made no claim to turn out Columbia Men recog-nizable—like Princeton or Yale Men—at twenty paces in a country-club bar. I am not sure this omission was a good thing; it must account, at least in part, for the relatively low solidarity my class showed after graduation. Instead of shared ideals, there was enormous diversity among us, and unlimited freedom for unrelated types to consort.

One other feature of the place strikes me in retrospect. It is customary nowadays to deplore the abandonment of un-dergraduate teaching by the senior faculty. They are said to be too busy with research grants, committees, and other ceremonious rituals to attend to College teaching, which, it seems, is turned over to the junior faculty with detrimental results. This is accepted as an established trend, so that it is surprising to discover that most of the courses offered in the College around 1937 were taught by instructors, not even by assistant professors. It is only fair to point out that the roster of instructors then included names like Hadas, Nagel, and Trilling, and a score of others equally notable. There were giants in those days.

Low Memorial Indeed

※⁂⁂⁂※

by Max Frankel

Lovely soul, lousy setting. A warm, snug life and a cold, ugly campus. Kind men teaching, crusty men administering. President Ike, even then, too short for his pedestal; Alma Mater too smug for hers. They painted on her patina one day, to match the rooftops of Hartley and Jay—very fake venerability in a place that always lived for the moment.

Trustees planning for the future and alumni reminiscing about the past were always bores.

The alumnus bores because he pretends that a unique memory represents a social experience. But when Mills and Miner, Van Doren and Hadas, Chiappe and Krutch and

MAX FRANKEL, *1952 College, 1953 M.A. in Public Law and Government, helps cover Washington—and thereby the world —as correspondent for the New York* Times.

Barger and Gutmann were done with me, they had loosed merely one more vanity upon the world that rebels against reunion. So why look back at all? Because the memory evokes a social experience. In each unanchored Hamilton chair a personality is exhumed, a value is confirmed, an attitude is firmly fixed.

My years at Columbia coincided with Ike's. The General addressed the beanies, freshman to freshman, he said, about moral rectitude and spiritual rededication. "I don't care how much they talk to you about geology and geography," he added. "I hope the day never goes by that you don't have some fun." Four years later, on Commencement Day, he was off saving and amusing the nation.

We watched him grow, from hero to saint, while he ran the place into the ground. Low Memorial indeed.

When in town, Wednesday mornings he would inspect the academic ranks. Andrew Chiappe was introduced as our Shakespearean four Wednesdays in a row and the General was delighted to meet him, every time. Between visits to the intellectual battlefield, he toured the alumni flanks. He had better luck with their names, especially golfing Texans who gave him five political dollars for every educational one. American Assembly hurrah.

Columbia was all that poor Ike ever knew of free enterprise. While temporarily off the Army's socialized medicine, he boned up on economic theory and urged us not to build our careers around Social Security. In his most memorable address, to a champagne and caviar banquet, he proclaimed the discovery that wholesome Americans were satisfied with beer and hot dogs. He was the filter tip of his day, and Columbia made him.

Who made him? The maker of great business machines. The keeper of great vaults. The seller of great books. The publisher of a great newspaper. Trustees: confined men, trusted to roam the grounds. Howard Fast was too dangerous to speak on our campus but Dwight Eisenhower was fit to lead it. Therein lay the genius of our tutors. Before the great push-ball melée on South Field in sophomore year we had become the equals of our betters. Before our first panty raid as juniors we had outgrown the ethic of our campus universe. The inner satisfaction and confidence may not have shown, but they were enough to climb mountains with. We had become the first AntiIke.

They wrote about us everywhere, mistakenly as the "silent" generation.

Yellowed inside my yearbook lies *The New York Times Magazine* of the week we were given our diplomas. The main article is about France having a tiger by the tail in Vietnam, finding it "as dangerous to hold on as to let go," but that is all about geology and geography. The important article was done on Morningside and it is called "The Terribly Normal Class of '52." The cowed curia of our faculty said the class was "more passive in the aggregate than its immediate predecessor." A distinguished dean said we were "singularly lacking in high spirits and enthusiasm." Our interviewer found us looking on the world with "sad resignation and incurable hope." Our goals were "modest and practical." We seemed to him sober without being earnest, quizzical rather than questioning, strong-minded and sophisticated, a likable lot, disarmingly frank and surprisingly urbane.

"Its vice," he concluded, "is an almost excessive balance,

an overpowering care not to commit its emotions too deeply to anything."

Well, Presidents come and go, but men of excessive balance live forever. Columbia, in her homely, clumsy way, could teach a raw recruit to despise the Commander in Chief but not to commit his emotions too deeply to anything. Alma Mater, fostering mother, she would willingly destroy herself for the enrichment of her sons.

All men of excessive balance should rejoice that for a mere $200 million we can repair the damage and carry on.

I Am Introduced
to Civilization

※﹒﹢﹒﹢﹒﹢﹒﹢﹒﹢﹒※

by Lloyd Frankenberg

In those days (I was originally class of 1928) the turnover
from high school to college was signalized by a change from
knickers to long trousers. Since today even a toddler of two
would scorn knickers, this is a part of ancient history. I
doubt if knickers are made any more, except perhaps highly
specialized ones for hunters, golfers, or baseball teams.

At our first arrival on campus we were herded into the
Chapel and given a serious talk on our new status. We were
now no longer boys, we were told; we were now young men.
We should behave accordingly. While we were to enjoy new

LLOYD FRANKENBERG *was a College student from 1924 to
1929, has written and recorded poetry, mused about poetry
in many a book and article, and has won a garland of fellowships, awards, and grants.*

liberties—for example, a number of cuts were to be allowed for each course—a certain decorum was to be expected of us. We were entering the mainstream of life.

Part of this entrance was to be inducted into a compulsory course with the resounding title of Introduction to Contemporary Civilization. (Do frosh still wear those little caps, which they have to tip to upperclassmen while addressing the latter as "sir"?)

Our class met at 9 A.M. I was always early, since for the first semester I commuted from out of town. But despite this relatively early hour for sleep-prone Columbia College men, quite a few others were in the habit of arriving ahead of time.

The instructor was young, dapper, and popular, and succeeded in making the rather conglomerate nature of the course—part history, part civics, part philosophical speculation—reasonably palatable. But this was not the only reason for the prompt, almost premature, attendance.

The instructor never got over his surprise, on entering, at finding the blackboard denuded of its usual paraphernalia of chalk and board erasers. Nearly every morning he had to send out for fresh supplies. It remained a complete mystery to him until that memorable morning when a beetle-browed, red-faced Dean burst into the room.

Even at normal times, Dean Herbert Hawkes possessed an air of severity for so short and plump a man. He had the reputation of being a strict disciplinarian. This day he was in a state that can only be described as high dudgeon.

"Will all those young gentlemen who have been in the habit of raining objects from this classroom please raise their hands?"

There was a moment of uneasy inactivity. He went on, trying to control his voice, "My wife reports she has just been struck by a board eraser. She tells me it came from one of these windows."

The uneasy silence prevailed. But it was plain that the cat was out of the bag. It had been the daily custom of nearly all of us prospective young civilians to foregather at one or another of the classroom's large windows facing on 116th Street and Amsterdam Avenue. Unsuspecting passers-by were greeted by a barrage whose aim increased in lethal accuracy from day to day. Nursemaids with baby carriages were especially desirable targets, since it was hard for them to get quickly out of range.

"If the culprits will not reveal themselves," continued the Dean, "I shall have to hold the whole class in jeopardy."

This threat, ambiguous as it was, did not fall short of the mark. If there were any nonindulgers in this indoor-outdoor sport, they were few and far between. What would happen to us all, if nebulous, was ominous. After another brief hesitation, three pairs of hands rose to the bait.

Were we excessively courageous, or more timid than the rest? Was it class loyalty that prompted us, or had we expected everyone else to be equally self-incriminating?

Whatever the case, we were ceremoniously ushered to the door. The rest of the class gazed after us, some with guilt, others with scorn.

Since the classroom was on the top floor, and we were in the august presence of the Dean, we had the inestimable privilege of descending, instead of by way of the broad staircase, by the one small elevator. This was a prerogative ordinarily reserved to members of the faculty. I doubt if any of us appreciated the signal honor.

All the way down I was thinking furiously, if my frantic inner process could truly be described as thought. How could we possibly propitiate our unspeaking, grim-set host?

On the ground floor we were led into that sanctum of sanctums, the Dean's office. Like all faculty offices in Hamilton Hall, it was devoid of all except a desk, a deal bookcase, and a few chairs. Probably, if I had had the temerity to glance about the tan walls, I would have found framed diplomas attesting to the academic standing of the distinguished occupant. But I was too busy to look anywhere except in the direction of the Dean.

Before the latter had had the chance to launch into the tirade he had undoubtedly been rehearsing during our slow and hushed, if creaky, descent, I found myself appointing myself spokesman for our little scared group. I am sure I cleared my throat nervously before delivering the choice conciliatory remarks I had been feverishly improvising.

"I wish you to know, Dean Hawkes," I said in the most respectful tones I could muster, "that had we known it was Mrs. Hawkes, we would certainly not have thrown a board eraser at her."

Perhaps it was the florid, though thoroughly correct, use of the subjunctive that did it. I am more inclined to think it was the utter inanity of my words. Or some combination of both. For whatever reason, the Dean's face momentarily cracked, like a pond at the approach of spring. If he did not exactly laugh out loud—he was seldom known to do that— it was plain that the back of his dignity was broken.

Quickly regaining his composure, he launched into a short,

pithy dissertation on propriety, courtesy, and the correct behavior of college men, particularly Columbia College men. But his heart was not quite in it. Continually, as he spoke, his eyes kept returning to me, and he could not conceal a certain recurrent, if fleeting, gleam. In the most unpredictable way in the world, I had somehow saved the day.

"Gentlemen," he concluded, "for this one occasion, I shall not put your names down in my little black book. But I am sure you will see to it that there will be no recurrence of this —er—type of activity."

Needless to say, from that day forward the blackboard in our classroom remained abundantly supplied with its appropriate materials. Citizens traversing 116th Street or Amsterdam Avenue no longer had to scurry for their lives. We had, far more than from any textbook or illustrated lecture, been introduced into what was, at least for that particular time and age, contemporary civilization.

Memories of
Goatville Days

꙳꙳꙳꙳

by H. R. Steeves

My memories of Columbia must seem today all but prehis-
toric, for I was a freshman in 1899. The University had
moved to Morningside only four years before—to the site
vacated by the old Bloomingdale Insane Asylum. Mr. Spencer
(I underscore the *Mr.*), white-whiskered curator of the
grounds, and a carry-over from Asylum days, still spoke of
the undergraduates as "inmates." Two buildings from the era
of mental disturbance still stood, and were used for classrooms. But the promise of a great future lay in six brand new

H. R. STEEVES, *1903 College, 1904 M.A., 1913 Ph.D., stayed
on at Columbia, beginning as assistant in English and becoming a professor emeritus, and at the same time writing
books and articles ranging from fiction through scholarship
and to such subjects as taxation.*

structures—the distinguished Low Library, and Fayerweather, Schermerhorn, Havemeyer, Engineering, and University halls, the last then and always uncompleted. South
Field was no more than purchasable real estate—and how
the University hungered for the money (wasn't it only a
million and a quarter?) necessary to buy it. From the campus
buildings one looked across open space to the lordly Hudson;
for there was not a single intervening building on the blocks
between 116th Street and 119th. The 115th–116th Street
block west of Broadway contained only two fraternity houses
on twenty-five-foot frontages. Where the Law School and
Johnson stand today there was a ledge of native rock ten or
twelve feet above the street level, and north of 120th Street
there was more of it, topped by dilapidated squatter shanties
here and there, with niches of grass browsed over by goats.
The familiar name of the neighborhood had been in actual
fact "Goatville." On the block on which Union Theological
has stood for many years there was just one two-story building, which had age and a bit of Georgian grace—the College
Tavern. It was not out of bounds for undergraduates, but it
was an unsavory place, and the most staid of us just wouldn't
be seen there. The El still rumbled overhead on Columbus
Avenue; the first spadeful of earth for the subway system had
not been dug; and horse cars rolled on both Amsterdam Avenue and Broadway. Coaches and barouches were driven along
Riverside Drive on sunny afternoons, with once in a great
while an electric coupe or hansom, still novel enough to be
regarded by New Yorkers of the Henry James school as rather
bad form.

Our instructors were notably gentlemen, generally young,
but some of them even then with touches of intellectual great-

ness. There were Brander Matthews, with his thin crop of whiskers, the quiet but very popular Woodberry, George Clinton Densmore Odell (whose name matched his classic countenance and stature), Nelson McCrea, Clarence Young, both classicists, Cassius Kayser, a mathematician whose complete involvement in his generally unfavored subject could on occasion fascinate even the dullest, William T. Shotwell, beatifically human and large-minded, and the aged Ogden Rood, professor of physics, whose magisterial ways invited the only undergraduate ragging from which I remember any of the professorial staff to have suffered. Those were the men appointed to work on our freshman minds, better, perhaps, most of those men, than the situation called for.

We entered with a class of about 150. We graduated, I think, about ninety. Among us freshmen were Carleton Hayes, Bob Schuyler, Dino Bigongiari (all of whom were to spend their entire lives at Columbia), George Warren and Marcy Dodge (to become in time trustees), and we turned out lawyers, doctors, business executives of the first water, financiers, congressmen, publishers, and writers. Our undergraduate idol was Harold Weekes, one of the great running and defensive halfbacks of all time. We were still drawing then on traditional Columbia families, some of them identified with the College since its foundation. But we had no dorms, and the "nice boys" had begun to show an increasing preference for the residence colleges. The University president in 1899 was Seth Low, who resigned within two years of our coming to become mayor of New York, and was succeeded by Nicholas Murray Butler.

I cannot pretend that we were all "inflamed with the study of learning." Indeed, I suspect that we had more than our quota of drop-outs—agreeable chaps who just could not hold the nose to a book. Yet we were products of a rather stern classical discipline. Almost all of us had entered on Latin, and continued it for at least another year. Between forty and fifty sat in the two sections of freshman Greek, which was brightened up even to the point of amusement by an experiment in colloquial instruction. I have a sharp recollection that the two most familiar responses in the classroom were οὐκ οἶδα and οὐ καταλαμβάνω (which we can translate for you ignorant moderns as "I don't know" and "I don't understand"). But we did turn out some undeniably important men.

Eighteen or twenty of us got around to our sixtieth anniversary commencement in 1963. Some good fruit still hangs on the old tree, and perhaps some of us are beginning to feel that one of us may survive to be hailed "oldest living graduate." It could be a pleasant distinction, but not untouched by nostalgia.

Thoreau, Columbia, and the World

༞࿔༺✦༻࿔༞

by Joseph Wood Krutch

Henry Thoreau once said that he had been born on the most favored spot on earth—and just in the nick of time, too. When I look back on my student years in the Columbia Graduate School of English I am tempted to exclaim something very much like that. It was a wonderful place to be at that moment and I can't help thinking that a very lucky chance brought me there just then.

I did not at the time know there was anything very special about the moment. I suppose I thought it had always been something like that around Philosophy Hall and that it always would be.

JOSEPH WOOD KRUTCH, *1916 M.A. and 1923 Ph.D., 1955 Litt.D., pre-eminent in American criticism, letters, and life for more than forty years, turned his back on the city and found his Concord at Tucson.*

But of course nothing ever is the same for long and never can be. Something is usually lost even though more is gained. And so it certainly was in this case. Philosophy Hall is busier than it was then. Its faculty is no less distinguished and I expect that the entering students are often better prepared as well as more sophisticated than most of us were in 1915. But inevitably something has also been lost, something which cannot be recaptured but for which compensations can and must be found.

Am I merely indulging in the romantic nostalgia of the aged, looking back on their youth and projecting upon the world what only their own free vigor, enthusiasm, and hope created? I do not think it is merely that. When I entered in 1915 the war that was about to bring the end of an era was still something that concerned the United States merely as a threat, not an actuality. This of course was one of the reasons why "just in the nick of time" is so appropriate a phrase. We might have been anxious about our own futures but we were not, as every thoughtful person now is, anxious about the future of the human race. And to be able to say that is to say a great deal about the fortunate condition of a graduate student of English in 1915.

But that is not all. There were reasons why Philosophy Hall itself was an especially favored spot. It was—if I may use the word—cozy, partly just because it was small. Almost without exception all candidates for the doctorate were acquainted with one another and for the most part they had frequent, informal contacts. There were, as far as I know, none who felt out of it. To be a doctoral candidate was (to use a fashionable word) to have an identity. We knew what our task was and we believed it worth accomplishing. Perhaps the fact that science and technology had not yet come, as now they have, to be so generally regarded as the only important subjects of study had something to do with it. We had full confidence in the legitimacy of our calling.

Only because our number was small could we know our teachers in just the way that we did know them. I do not mean that we were on a familiar basis. Indeed I suspect that we held a professor in much greater awe than is usually the case today. But they were very much persons nevertheless— not merely figures on the lecture platform or at the seminar table. And what a variety of vivid personalities there was! I am sure that every member of our small group remembered always (to mention only the seniors) the magisterial decisiveness of Ashley Thorndike, the jaunty worldliness of Brander Matthews, the old-fashioned poise of William Peterfield Trent, and the shy elegance of W. W. Lawrence. Now all of even the juniors are gone except for Hunter Wright, who was to succeed Ashley Thorndike. What we learned from them about human nature and the rich variety of possibilities within its limits was, I think, almost as important as anything they taught us about their scholarly specialties. I suppose that a mathematician or a physicist may learn all he needs to know from textbooks and laboratories, but a humanist needs to know things which only contact with other human beings can teach him. Most of us were young men with a pretty limited experience of the world. Just to observe men of much greater experience—as well as of great eminence—was an important part of our education.

That we were a coherent, special group, but also a part of a great metropolis, seemed to me then, and still seems to me now, to have given us an advantage over those whose academic community is isolated from the world. Though I decided a good many years ago that I had had enough of cities, I have never doubted that some experience with them is nearly indispensable to a full intellectual development. At some time in the course of his development every man should rub shoulders with his fellows, have some experience with the excitement of a city's nervous activities, live close enough to the great, the distinguished, and the merely notorious—if for no other reason than merely because only so can he learn to discount them properly or to distinguish between them. Without having lived for a time in a metropolis it is not likely that he will ever fully escape some trace of provinciality.

That advantage Columbia will always willy-nilly enjoy. The conditions that seemed to be so desirable can never be recovered, any more than Thoreau's Concord can be recovered. This is a different world and it must therefore be a different Columbia. The danger is simply that it might be compelled to accept the disadvantages of the modern world without being able to enjoy its opportunities. I hope the means will be found to enable it to take full advantage of the latter. It would make me very unhappy to think that future generations of students would not have something to look back upon with pleasure as great as that with which I look back upon the old Columbia.

The First of the Great

by Richard B. Snow

I went to Columbia as an accommodation to my family. I knew nothing of the College, or of any college except Stanford, a warm boyhood memory on the other side of the continent. By now my western loyalties were dim. I loved New York; I loved music; I didn't want anything to change.

But people in my family were supposed to go to college. I was not restless about my very unacademic life, but my father (how well I understand it now) was beginning to be. In February of 1922 I sat for the psychological examination

RICHARD B. SNOW, *1926 College, 1931 B.Arch., has been practicing architecture in New York City for more than thirty-seven years. He is a past president of the School of Architecture Alumni Association, and has been active for a long time in University alumni affairs.*

in the big gymnasium, bought a little blue cap, and registered for Columbia College at six dollars a point.

My first impressions were of monumental cast-iron bank architecture, a great deal of golden oak seating, and some organized scuffles about the little blue cap. Things came into focus when I went to my first class, which was the big gun of the freshman year, styled euphoniously Contemporary Civilization.

A very slight, very blond young man came into the classroom at a brisk trot. Even to freshmen he seemed young. His appealing gaze was without focus, directed nowhere, but he got right to work. He told us his name was Irwin Edman. Already we sensed that ours was the lucky section.

We were to learn that under forced draft Dr. Edman himself had created our textbook *Human Traits and Their Social Significance*. He was a philosopher by profession, a master of comparative religion, a probing student of the fine arts. Blessed with a remarkable gift of total recall for prose and poetry, he came to the classroom unencumbered with notebooks and texts, delivering beautifully organized lectures in a sweet and rather quiet voice. Although he was not unaccustomed to toying with a piece of chalk from time to time, no elaborate outlines or briefs were ever committed to the blackboard. A discussion of the prolonged period of infancy in the human race and its ultimate effect on human characteristics might be memorialized on the board by the word "baby." Once I listened to a presentation of some aspect of intuitive knowledge; it may have been in connection with the philosophy of Henri Bergson, which Dr. Edman characterized as "the difference between dissecting a frog and being one."

The blackboard outline of this concept was the single tiny word "frog" in crabbed script. But we remembered, and we loved him.

One of Irwin Edman's duties in Contemporary Civilization was to impart to us (this was forty-odd years ago) the idea that there were many other religions than the one in which any of us may have grown up. There was the Christian God, the God of the Old Testament, the scientific god—more remote, less anthropomorphic. He developed this theme at length with earnestness, with tact. To me, and I remember it vividly, these ideas, offered by this man, obviously sincere, obviously good, came not as a disturbance but as a release and a stimulus.

All through the term he tossed ideas at us, helped us to grow accustomed to them, to live with them. Contemporary Civilization was very broad-spectrum, very rousing to a group of freshmen most of whose experience with thought was just beginning. Later in life I came to understand something of the great knowledge, the creative imagination that Dr. Edman drew on for these daily discussions of history, psychology, anthropology, and religion. At the time it all seemed effortless; not indifferent, just wonderfully effortless. How Olympian our perspective began to seem to us under this gentle guidance. It was great for Columbia. With ideas, with teachers like these, what college, we all thought, could compare with this one. I was glad I had stayed in the East.

Irwin Edman was the first of the great teachers I was destined to have at Columbia, the living demonstration on the opening day that nothing was too great to be hoped for from this faculty on Morningside. He was a brilliant and versatile man and lived a very full life outside the University as writer, critic, lecturer, and traveler. His books were charming. So many fields were open to him. How grateful we are that he never forsook his finest role—teacher at Columbia.

Politics and Football

❧❀❀❀❀❀

by James A. Wechsler

The striking thing is how vivid are so many recollections
of that interval on Morningside Heights from September 1931
to June 1935. It must have been "the best of times and the
worst of times"; it is hard to recall a dull moment, except for
certain classroom agonies in such mystery domains as astronomy, which I flunked. But many classes were out of this world
to those, like myself, who spent most of their undergraduate
careers working on the *Columbia Spectator* and engaging
in the radical upheavals that intermittently disrupted the campus.

Much of the story of that era has been written earlier by

JAMES A. WECHSLER, *1935 College, started on* Spectator,
went on to the Nation *and* PM, *and has his say every day as
editor of the editorial page of the New York* Post.

myself and others. Perhaps one uncommon aspect of my experience was the struggle between my political involvement and my seemingly congenital addiction to sports, especially football. Although my playing career ended on a sandlot, my grandstand emotions have never subsided.

But things weren't simple. My first autumn at Columbia was Lou Little's second season and the real beginning of the glory years. Still fresh in memory is the day of our conquest of Dartmouth (which had defeated us 52–0 the previous year). An especially powerful figure in that triumph was a square-shouldered, pugnacious end.

Those triumphs of Saturday's heroes, however, were shadowed by the simultaneous campaign being waged by *Spectator* editor Reed Harris against what he viewed as the crass "overemphasis" on football—and loose recruiting standards —that had allegedly accompanied Little's advent. As a freshman member of the *Spectator* staff, and one who had committed himself to a crusading journalist's life at the age of about ten, the Harris strictures came as a depressive sequel to each satisfaction of Saturday at Baker Field.

The complexity became almost intolerable when, in April 1932, Harris was expelled (not for his anti-football crusade but rather, it was indicated, for his exposure of certain malpractice in the management of the dining halls). There ensued the student strike and, alas, as one of the reporters assigned to the day's tumult, I came upon a scene in which the aforementioned fiery hero of the Dartmouth encounter seemed bent upon pushing the pipe of Rob Hall, one of the leading student leftists—later to become a full-time Communist functionary—down his throat. (I cannot swear that he was unprovoked.) But this was to be only the first of many occasions on which some gridiron stalwarts felt obliged to perform combat duty against the legions of the Left who were besmirching "the good name of the University."

Throughout my undergraduate years this ambivalence in my relationship to the football squad—or at least many of its members—inevitably persisted. Amid all the recurrent clashes of that time in which (as I viewed it) the athletic forces were repeatedly mobilized on the side of super-patriotism, I nevertheless found myself drawn compulsively to Baker Field on Saturday and frenetically cheering the very men who might be hurling eggs at me the following week when I delivered an historic antiwar oration (or some variation thereof) from that Hyde Park of Columbia known as the Sun Dial.

As I became increasingly persuaded that the Marxist simplicities of history contained the only true answers to the perils and frustrations of our time, I did achieve a certain reconciliation in my conflict of interests. For the truth was that some—perhaps many—of the stalwarts of Columbia's new gridiron age were being recruited from the mining towns of western Pennsylvania and other key industrial regions. These were the true sons of the working class; while they seemed coldly indifferent or truculently hostile to the Marxist message of liberation being addressed to them, one could hardly dismiss them as tools of American imperialism or regard them as intruders.

There came, then, the critical moment when Little's legions gained their ultimate eminence—an invitation to the Rose Bowl. *Spectator*, on which I was then an active candidate for the editorship, denounced the acceptance of the bid as a surrender to the crass commercialization of the Pasadena profiteers. I publicly defended the paper's stand; it was with an almost furtive manner that I listened joyously to the radio report of the unforgettable triumph over Stanford.

Someone has remarked caustically that I devoted myself as an undergraduate to subverting Columbia's participation in the Rose Bowl and have spent most of my adult years dreaming of a comparable invitation. This, I must insist, is an oversimplification of the tortuously conflicting emotions I suffered. But, if it was indeed a sin to identify with Reed Harris' anti-football aggressions, I have surely atoned by now through long years of faithful presence on tragic Saturdays.

If there is an aspect of frivolity in this reminiscence, it is induced by a certain self-consciousness about my sentimentality about Columbia. Perhaps the most withering remark my wife (a Barnard girl whom I married while we both were still undergraduates) has ever addressed to me came during a characteristically sad Columbia-Princeton game of recent years when my anguish became both transparent and strident. Suddenly I heard her saying, "James, you really have become an old grad." I should add that I am addressed as "James" (rather than Jimmy) only when my conduct is peculiarly aberrant.

It wasn't all political fun and football games. We who entered Columbia that fall of 1931 had reason to look at the world in perhaps the same way that some young undergraduates are seeing it now. The Depression was a central fact of life for us; the racial crisis has comparably explosive overtones now. The war and threats of war filled the air; now there are Vietnam and the hydrogen bomb.

Even for those of us whose homes somehow survived the economic crisis, there was a sense of guilt; it was not too far from Morningside Heights to that spectacle of ultimate human indignity known as the bread line. And some of us went to see it.

There were voices among us who said there was a simple formula for salvation; it was known as Marxism-Leninism and its tenets were being practiced in a country called the Soviet Union. The virtues of this experiment were advertised to us by a couple of our instructors (whose dismissal during my undergraduate days provided the signal for what became our annual spring strikes). But they are hardly the villains of the piece.

The fact is that there was a vast wasteland of skepticism and despair, and their dogmas filled the vacuum.

For most of us the damage did not prove to be fatal. I hardly look back with pride to an edition of *Spectator* I edited which carried a page-one cartoon showing Dr. Butler beating babies (he had recently testified against the child-labor amendment). But neither is this presented as a contrite confessional.

Far better a live campus than a dead one; better a campus on which there was the symphony of discordant debate rather than monolithic muteness; better a campus that so many of us now remember as a battleground than a graveyard; better a campus that seethed with controversy about man's fate than one that offered the illusion of escape. Those of us who thought we had found what Adlai Stevenson once called "quick and easy" solutions were wrong; but we were right in recognizing the apocalyptic nature of the times. Too many of my classmates died on beachheads at Anzio and other places in confirmation of our often grim warnings to the comfortable.

Possibly, too, those of us who eventually escaped from

dogma without abandoning concern are more indebted than we know to those who patiently heard us out and volunteered a quiet, unprovocative challenge to our certitudes. Still clear in memory is the image of Irwin Edman, in the soft twilight in Philosophy Hall, trying to remind "dialectical materalists" of the beauty in nature that transcends class war, and William Casey artfully undermining the cliches of Marxism (and other fanaticisms), and Bob Carey pleading for reason against self-righteousness. There were others who similarly suffered our intolerances and gave us the supreme, if sometimes unwarranted, grace of being taken seriously because they shared our unease. At the risk of romanticism, I like to think that those years helped to strengthen the atmosphere of diversity that pervades Columbia, and that sustains some semblance of communication with another troubled—and sometimes trying —generation.

Forty-three Years
of Columbia

※ ⁂ ※

by Paul R. Hays

When I look back on these many years at Columbia, forty-three now, with only two brief interruptions, my mind is suffused with a host of memories. I suppose there are few who knew, as I did, those giants of an even then outdated classical training: Nelson Glenn McCrea, Frank Gardner Moore, and Edward Delavan Perry. Perry, who was the oldest of the group, was Jay Professor of Greek. He had immense learning as well as a kind of puckish playfulness which I can illustrate by a story about one of his exploits. Perry had a

---

PAUL R. HAYS, *1925 College, 1927 A.M., 1933 Law, has taught Greek, Latin, and Law at Columbia, practiced law, served city, state, and nation on countless legal and political fronts, and is United States Judge, United States Court of Appeals for the Second Circuit.*

typewriter which could be changed from the Roman alphabet to the Greek. Frequently, with professorial absent-mindedness, he would forget to shift types and would find that he had typed a page or two of English in Greek letters or a page or two of Greek in Roman letters. So he composed a short poem in ancient Greek to paste on the typewriter, the burden of which was designed to remind him to shift to the appropriate type. A native devilishness led him one day to approach several of the younger members of the department with copies of his poem and to inquire gravely whether they could help him to identify in Greek literature the source of the verses. You will realize that, not knowing the purpose of the verses, the young instructors had considerable difficulty fathoming their meaning, to say nothing of the difficulty of locating them in the corpus of Greek poetry.

I was one of those young instructors. Some of you may remember two of the others, H. Theodoric Westbrook, who died many years ago, and Moses Hadas, who himself went on to a distinguished career as Jay Professor of Greek and whose tragic death was reported only recently.

I did some of my teaching in Barnard College, and since I was only twenty-two when I started to teach I was, I am afraid, a bit victimized by the girls in my classes at Barnard. I recall a class in the poetry of Catullus. To show off a bit I had assigned as our textbook the Teubner edition of Catullus, a text which contained his complete poems without any notes except textual notes. One day early in the term, quite unwarily, I assigned the next ten or so pages without looking ahead. When I got around to preparing my lesson I found to my horror that I had assigned one of Catullus' most obscene poems. There was nothing that I could do about it then, so when I got to class I announced that we would skip that poem. "Oh no we won't," said my class of Barnard girls. "You assigned it and we have worked on it. We want to read it." You may think that it was the girls who did the blushing. But it was not.

One of the nonclassical professors I remember best was John Erskine. He used to play the piano from time to time to illustrate points in his lectures. I shall never forget his demonstrations of how the language of *Hamlet* was pronounced in Shakespeare's day. On one occasion after I had begun to teach classics I was riding up in the elevator at Hamilton Hall with Erskine. He said to me, "Why doesn't one of you fellows write a book making Helen of Troy out to be a modern day flapper?" (Even the word has an old-fashioned ring!) I laughed and replied that I couldn't believe that such a book would have much of an audience. A few months later there appeared *The Private Life of Helen of Troy* by John Erskine. And as you well recall the book was a best seller for many weeks.

One of the few professors we had in College who is still living is Mark Van Doren. He stands out in my memory not so much as brilliant teacher but as a quiet, gentle man clothed in a mantle of modesty.

Still thinking of the English department, the dullest and most inept teacher I ever had anywhere was one who also wrote a best seller and a very exciting one—Hervey Allen, who wrote *Anthony Adverse*. He was so completely without imaginative resources as a teacher that he spent many class hours reading to his students from the textbook that they had in their hands.

Among our other teachers was John Dewey, whose teaching methods influenced so profoundly the so-called progressive education with which our children had to deal. His own teaching method was *sui generis*. He would wander around the room stopping from time to time to look out the window or to examine a picture on the wall. Occasionally he would say something. When he did so he appeared to be talking to himself and rarely were his remarks relevant to anything the class was supposed to be considering. But with all this there was an air of greatness about Dewey that left his classes considerably in awe of him.

Four Historic Years

ᵇᵉ᱖ᵉᵉᵉᵉ᱖ᵉ

by M. Lincoln Schuster

A backward glance is traditionally taken through rose-colored glasses. This is particularly true when the past is recaptured on a memorable and dramatic anniversary. Since my class at Columbia University—the Class of 1917—celebrated its semi-centennial last year, I plead guilty on fifty counts—one for each year—of unabashed sentimentality, and throw myself on the mercy of the court. In defense of this powerful emotional component in my recollections, I can only cry out in the immortal words of Al Smith, "Let's look at the record!"

When words have become as deeds, and dates have become

M. LINCOLN SCHUSTER, *1917 Journalism, started as a copyboy on the New York* Evening World, *was half the founding team of Simon & Schuster, and numbers among his associations the Wednesday Culture Club That Meets on Fridays.*

as events, the record assumes some valid historic impact, especially if it is summarized by years like 1913–14 and 1917, marking the range of my student years at Columbia University.

Our class was lucky beyond words to be at Morningside at a time packed tight with history-in-the-making. We enrolled in September 1913, and Sarajevo and the First World War were just around the corner. At the end of our freshman year, dynasties and empires were beginning to break up and the lights were going out all over Europe. America was becoming a world power and assuming the leadership held until then by England. When we were graduated in 1917, the American Expeditionary Forces were on their way to Flanders Field, fresh from the student training camps like Plattsburg. Revolutions were a dime a dozen—revolutions in politics, in nationalism, in science, in art, and in thought. Albert Einstein and Sigmund Freud were front-page news, and Karl Marx and H. G. Wells were promising brave new worlds.

This is the strongest ingredient in our remembrance. World history was not an academic abstraction—but an immediate experience, heightened by the realization that there were giants in those days on the Columbia University faculty.

Heading this group was that spectacular triumvirate— Robinson, Dewey, and Beard. They were my teachers, my heroes, my favorite humanists, sages, and advisers. I started my first year taking a combined course in Columbia College and the newly established Pulitzer School of Journalism. At the halfway mark, at the end of my second year, I shifted entirely to Journalism. The Class of 1917 was the first to take the full four-year course in Journalism. I therefore had the privilege of steeping myself in the humanities and the classics of world literature while preparing myself not just for a job, but for the profession and discipline of Journalism. The history of the intellectual class in Europe with James Harvey Robinson (I heard him announce his celebrated concept of "the humanization of knowledge"), philosophy with John Dewey (and a revolution in education), American history with Charles A. Beard (ushering in new and radical concepts in politics)—these were all "firsts" that shaped my studies and changed my life.

Other giants on the Columbia faculty at that time were John Erskine (whose honors seminars in literature marked the beginning of the courses in Contemporary Civilization and the Great Books program, later adopted by the Encyclopaedia Britannica), Walter B. Pitkin, who taught philosophy long before life began at forty (his lectures and seminars on the lives and the wisdom of the great thinkers inspired me ten years later to publish *The Story of Philosophy*), Edwin R. A. Seligman (who showed me that economics was *not* the dismal science), Dr. Talcott Williams, first director of the School of Journalism (who taught me the ground rules of reporting and editorial writing, as well as the structure and classification of all knowledge through the Dewey Decimal System), working city editors like Franklin Matthews of the *Sun* and Robert Emmett MacAlarney of the *Herald Tribune* (who conditioned us to write under pressure of a deadline and to strive passionately for "clean copy"), Edwin E. Slosson (who introduced us to "creative chemistry" and reconciled for us the two cultures of science and the humanities), John W. Cunliffe (who taught his students how to read a book and inspired me twenty years later to publish *A Treasury of the Theatre,* spanning the whole sweep from Aeschylus to Eugene O'Neill), as well as an entire faculty committed, in the words of Joseph Pulitzer, to the goals of "accuracy, terseness, accuracy."

My fellow students and contemporaries were also great teachers, many of them destined to become giants themselves in various creative fields. We were fortunate to be a small class of about forty members. We had no need for fraternities. We *were* a fraternity. Among my classmates or contemporaries were Morrie Ryskind (Pulitzer Prize winner for *Of Thee I Sing*), Howard Dietz (M.G.M. and "The Little Shows" that became big hits), George A. Hough, Jr. (editor-in-chief and publisher of the Falmouth *Enterprise*), Irwin Edman (author of *Human Traits,* and later, chairman of the Columbia University Philosophy Department), Oscar Hammerstein and Richard Rodgers (starting a new era in musical comedy at the other end of the campus), James Marshall (who became an eminent lawyer and president of the New York Board of Education), Donald M. Stern and Merryle S. Rukeyser (our first capitalists), George E. Sokolsky (who was railroaded out of the University and who, a few years later in China, bought the railroad), Elliott M. Sanger (founder of WQXR), William Hillman (who interviewed, syndicated, and did ghostwriting for President Truman), Henry Beetle Hough (editor of *The Vineyard Gazette,* known as "The Thunderer," and Pulitzer Prize winner), Bennett Cerf (two classes later, who entered the publishing field as replacement for Richard L. Simon at Liveright's, when Dick, also a Columbia graduate, left Liveright to form S & S with me in 1924), Alan Harrison Temple (financial editor and economist, and our first classmate to become a Columbia University trustee), Colonel Clarence Lovejoy (alumni director and author of *The Lovejoy*

College Guides, later launched by S & S), and other stellar names too numerous to mention.

Inspired by such teachers and such fellow students, I joined the working press in my sophomore year and became a correspondent, first for Columbia, and then for New York City, for the Boston *Evening Transcript,* the only metropolitan newspaper ever immortalized in a poem by T. S. Eliot.

My list of schoolmates, friends, heroes, and teachers could be expanded all the way from A to Z, except for the fact that at the School of Journalism I was taught to be brief. For me, this became a compulsion, an obsession, and eventually, as a book publisher, a commitment to "little books on big subjects." From Alfred North Whitehead I learned that as knowledge advances, it can be put into little books.

As a newspaper correspondent since my sophomore year I was doubly fortunate: first, I thus served my apprenticeship in journalism, and, second, my employment helped me work my way through Columbia. I was not content to *cover* the news, but as a member of a small but explosively unorthodox class, I participated in the *making* of news. When Morrie Ryskind referred to President Butler as Czar Nicholas in *The Columbia Jester* and was thereupon invited to leave the school, I covered the story for the Boston *Evening Transcript* blow by blow, together with exclusive statements from Morrie in the form of Horatian odes in Latin and English. When Journalism students were embattled with Columbia College students, in a student board election struggle, I gladly sacrificed my journalistic objectivity and won myself some exclusive stories at lucrative space rates. When Bertrand Russell lectured at Columbia in 1915 I attended as a student, and several years later became his American publisher, with *Unpopular Essays* and *A History of Western Philosophy.*

The first Simon and Schuster catalogue in 1924 listed books by Irwin Edman, Maxwell Anderson, and Merryle S. Rukeyser, as well as a biography of Joseph Pulitzer by Don C. Seitz. A few years after graduation I became an associate instructor on the Journalism faculty, and acted as assistant to Professor Walter B. Pitkin when he gave his famous course on The Psychology of News Interest. Professor Pitkin inspired me to collect examples of human error and folly, and thus gave me an idea for a book which we later asked Pitkin to write for S & S—a mammoth volume entitled *A Short Introduction to the History of Human Stupidity.*

In my discussions and seminars with philosophers like Irwin Edman I learned to read and revere the great sages and humanists of all time, and as a result became a lifelong compulsive collector of "short sentences based on long experience." This will be the foundation for a series I am now planning on The Wisdom of the (S)Ages. My first pilot volume will be *The Wisdom of Montaigne,* which now has top priority on my editorial drawing board. Later will follow *The Wisdom of Goethe, The Wisdom of Cervantes, The Wisdom of Plato, The Wisdom of Pascal, The Wisdom of The Bible, The Wisdom of The Talmud, The Wisdom of Thomas Jefferson, The Wisdom of Emerson, The Wisdom of Thoreau,* and more than fifty others—all going back to editorial researches I started as a student at Columbia. In fact, I can clearly and gratefully recall the first "short sentence based on long experience" that sparked what H. G. Wells called the "research magnificent." It was an aphorism of

Emerson's on the basic fallacy of wealth and material possessions: "My cow milks me." I became an expert on experts
—recalling the famous definition of an expert: "A man who
avoids all the small errors as he sweeps on to the grand
fallacy."

This brings me back to my opening theme on the historic
and intellectual climate of Columbia University during the
four historic years from 1913 to 1917. To be alive then was
an adventure unparalleled. To be young and to sit at the feet
of teachers who were true giants, and to fraternize with
fellow students who acted as a committee on new traditions—
especially with tuition fees then scaled at only $5.00 a point
—all this was for me the ultimate in life enhancement.

A Student Was
One Who Studied

by Herbert Brucker

An October dusk was settling over Broadway and 116th. Through the windows of the fifth-floor newsroom in the Journalism Building a straying eye could see, beyond the dark buildings across the street, orange clouds over New Jersey. To at least one student it was a good time of year, and an interesting prospect lay ahead.

This student, unlike many of his classmates, was a stranger to journalism. Some of those at the typewriter tables around him had edited their school or college papers. Others had even worked as professionals, reporters on real newspapers in

HERBERT BRUCKER, *1924 Journalism, has been a reporter, a professor, an assistant to a dean, a writer, editor of the venerable Hartford* Courant, *and is Director of Professional Journalism Fellowships at Stanford.*

the world outside. But until recently it had not even occurred to him that he might at least have tried out for the *East Orange High School News,* or the *Williams Record.* Almost by accident he found himself in Columbia's School of Journalism, to see whether newspapers might be the career for him.

That day, at the opening of class, Professor Charles Phillips Cooper—Coop, when he wasn't within earshot—had handed back the previous assignments. Across the top of the neophyte's neatly folded copy, dutifully left blank for the imaginary headline to come, four or five big red X's had been streaked on with a fat wax pencil. This was the Red Apple— Coop's familiar trademark to generations of students at Columbia's School of Journalism. It signified a job well done.

As a teacher, this short, round man with bristling mustache set in a red face might not get far today. He was a college graduate. He even had an honorary doctorate from his alma mater, Wesleyan. But he was innocent of any Ph.D. And presumably it hadn't occurred to him that compiling questionnaires and manipulating mathematical symbols was a prerequisite for teaching journalism. He had been a newspaperman. In his day he had run the news side of the *Evening Sun.* He was, moreover, an alumnus of the famous war desk of 1918's New York *Times,* all of whose members were said to have been managing editors elsewhere in their own right.

Among his other qualifications as a teacher of journalism Coop had a voice that could bark ferociously. This could have an overpowering effect on the new student. But, after a while, one learned that the bark was worse than the bite that never really came. The sudden twinkle in the brown eyes under those bushy eyebrows, the friendly grin that unexpectedly softened a face that incarnated the tales one heard of hard-boiled city editors, revealed the real man. But the combination worked. It prompted students to want a Red Apple, and to struggle to get it.

It is different now. Not only is the journalism teacher likely to wear on his brow that mark of the academic Brahmin, the Ph.D., but he is also likely to know less about getting out a newspaper than Charles P. Cooper. But then, students in those days were different too. In the early twenties there was always a scattering of wise guys in any student group. But most of us, though we were not to hear the term for a generation, were squares. We thought the students of Paris or Caracas or wherever, who took part in the politics of their country by marching in sometimes riotous demonstrations, were typically unstable citizens of comic-opera countries. To us a student was one who studied. His job was to prepare himself for life rather than to seek precociously to participate in it. So it seemed only natural to learn what one could from the older generation. One could always be certain of improving on that older generation when the time came to go out into the world and conquer it.

Other times, other customs. Certainly in the twenties there was little of today's kowtowing to the student, with the administration seemingly almost afraid of the students when in all history, despite the perennial rebelliousness of youth, it has been the other way around. Nor was there any of today's nonsense about the student's knowing better than his teachers what kind of education he should have.

Hindsight may see the academic climate in the Journalism Building of the twenties as more stable than it really was. Still, it was relatively easy then to absorb not only journalistic technics, and that all-inclusive background that is essential to newspaper work, but to acquire standards and principles as well. We learned about such things from Coop. Under his watchful authority we tried and tried again at our typewriters to qualify for the $25 a week we might soon hope to earn, during the blossoming boom of the twenties, in the big time outside.

Coop, of course, was by no means alone. The teaching staff was a heterogeneous crew of practitioners and scholars. Talcott Williams for one, who had been the first director of the school, was still about from time to time, though not formally instructing. From him one could learn of the analogy between the newspaperman and the Hebrew prophet that is implicit in verses one through nine of the thirty-third chapter of Ezekiel. It is an analogy that served well those who felt its meaning in their youth, and thereafter tried to apply it despite the harsh realities of journalism.

Just so the others in that variegated array, each in his own way, had something to offer. There was the director of the school, the English-born John W. Cunliffe, he of the velvet jacket and white goatee. I can still hear him sniffing knowledgeably, at the appropriate points, as he led us through D. H. Lawrence and the others in his courses on modern European fiction and modern European drama. Some among us did not rate him highly because his antecedents were scholarly, rather than acquired in the streets on assignments or at a desk in the newsroom. But there was background there, nonetheless. Background, always background.

Then there was Walter B. Pitkin, whose formal education had ended in a divinity degree from Yale, but who had things to say about the psychology of news interest, and about feature writing, that stood the test of practice. Or there was Roscoe Conkling Ensign Brown, he of the Phi Bete key and years in the musty sanctum of the New York *Tribune*. His lectures on politics made a foundation for those who were to find their way into political reporting or editorial writing.

Again, there was Colonel Sackett, with his incisive reduction of the infinite complexities of libel to practical rules for the reporter and copy reader. There was Max Schuster, of the fabulous journalism Class of 1917. He was then a correspondent for the Boston *Evening Transcript,* and a part-time lecturer on feature writing. The firm of Simon & Schuster was still but a dream in his head. So too there were Merryle S. Rukeyser and Alan H. Temple on financial writing. Both were also '17J, and both were to achieve distinguished careers. And there were others.

Out of it all, and out of the endlessly repeated drill of writing, writing, and writing, always subject to detailed and expert revision, one somehow acquired a whiff of that breadth and understanding, that discipline in finding words to fit the facts and the thoughts they are to convey, that form the bedrock of journalism. Indeed the goal in that less complicated day was much the same as one now set by Edward W. Barrett, dean of today's Graduate School of Journalism:

"The breadth of knowledge required to understand today's events, the skill to record and interpret them with polish and deftness, the integrity to do so with ruthless fairness, and the vision ultimately to seek and perhaps to find better ways to do the job."

As one turns to look back down the long corridor of the years one becomes the more aware of the changes men have made since those days at Broadway and 116th Street. Today's world seems peopled, more than that of long ago, by David Riesman's other-directed men. These are the ones who know the angles—the hip and the cool. They go about as though with radar sets on their heads, so that they may the more nimbly dodge the obstacles and the difficulties that were better met head on. This in contrast to the once more prevalent inner-directed specimen. Such a one acquires during his upbringing, in and out of school, a sense of moral direction. It is as though he had, deep in his system somewhere, a gyroscope that holds him to the course upon which he has been set, or upon which he has set himself.

However times and people may have changed, or not, the Journalism Building has changed little from that day to this. For more than a generation, to be sure, the fifth-floor newsroom has been transformed into the executive offices of the school. The first-floor newsroom has long since become the seminar chamber of the American Press Institute. But perhaps the intangibles remain what they were.

One hopes so, because those days were good. From them one learned, among other things, that journalism can be a calling as honorable, and as useful, as any—and more interesting than most.

Town and Gown

ᖵᖅᑎᖅᒃᖅᕿ

by H. L. Jacobson

My job in an intergovernmental organization is counseling the developing nations of Asia, Africa, and Latin America on their export trade, income from which is essential to their development and, in some cases, to their very survival.

In a very real sense I learned at Columbia how to do everything I am now doing, although thirty years of experience on five continents has taught me some additional techniques of applying the notions basically acquired on her beloved asphalt campus.

I refer not merely to my Columbia training in economics

H. L. JACOBSON, *1936 College, has roamed the world for more than three decades in various professional capacities, and now is Director of the International Trade Centre, General Agreement on Tariffs and Trade, at Geneva.*

and its sister sciences. Nevertheless, it was a privilege during the Great Depression to have professors—among them the future governor of Puerto Rico, who laid the groundwork for its present industrial boom—walk into the classroom sleepy-eyed straight from a Washington milk train and start the lecture by saying, "At dinner last night, the President asked me how we could. . . ." It made us feel (forever) that the "destiny" of the human race lies in human hands, especially those of its articulate minority who have had the good fortune of a university education and are, in consequence, sitting at the levers of communication—so that, by reverse implication, a breakdown *could* be blamed on a *trahison des clercs*.

But I am confident that, even without the inspiration of a national catastrophe, Columbia would have bred its sons to a comprehension of—and feeling for—liberty and justice (the one, sooner or later, unable to flourish without the other). Knowledge, as conceived at Columbia, is for social use as well as personal enjoyment. By the thirties it had become clear to any thinking man that, unless the intellectuals of the country applied themselves to setting straight the anarchy into which short-sighted economic egotism and cultural ivory towerism had plunged an overconfident nation, culture itself would soon be considered a mere mockery.

But, then, having recast our domestic mold, we found ourselves strung out across the world in a just, though avoidable, war. Coming out of that victoriously with hands stretching toward the laurel, we crossed other, darker, hands reaching out to us—one palm outstretched, the other balled up into a fist.

These were the hands of men I had already studied with

at Columbia, which has a melting-pot recruiting bias. (Today
my staff includes one economist from Peru and another from
Nigeria—both from Columbia, though a quarter of a century
after my time.) I do not refer only to such situations as having
had as a roommate the son of the deposed king of Kurdistan
(the son went on to become the courageously progressive
Minister of Transport of Iraq); or that, when a million
volumes had to be transferred from the old library to the
new, the fellow student next to me on the human chain that
did it was the son of a former premier of Haiti. I reckon that
from the days when that Scots Bermudan bastard, Alexander
Hamilton, chased the Royalist dean into the Hudson to get a
New World Unlimited started, Columbia has always considered culture and its application as universal. We never
had to be indoctrinated not to condescend to men with less
pale faces; on the contrary, we never thought of ourselves as
being, in any humanly significant way, different from them.

My class was particularly fortunate in its mentors. I had
Barzun and Trilling as instructors, then at the beginning of
what was already clear would be great careers, though they
were only a few years older than we. It would be presumptuous
of me to attempt to assess their intellectual merits, but I can
say something about them as teachers. Barzun's flashes of
insight (arising out of encyclopediac learning) blasted away
whole layers of stultifying preconceptions, while setting off
chain reactions in his students. His favorite target was[1]—and
is[2]—the new determinism in sociology as well as the natural
sciences. He riddled the pseudo-scientists who, starting from

[1] *Darwin, Marx, Wagner,* 1941.
[2] *Science: The Glorious Entertainment,* 1964.

the physical limitations in nature—including man's—go on to draw the conclusion that it is fatuous to breast the "wave of the future"—a doctrine inadmissible at Broadway and 116 Street.

He was a towering charismatic figure, who aroused the kind of fierce loyalties that the medieval masters must have, when their students, in their theological disputations, occasionally left a cadaver on the ground on dispersing. (Our disputes were over ideology, the modern theology.) Now, thirty years later, whenever I return to America, I still report to him regularly, with all the humility of a student; and still find my thinking on practical problems and their cultural— in the broad sense—consequences stimulated by his cut and thrust.

Trilling, chugging calmly at his pipe, his hair prematurely white with the weight of the world, impressed on us the moral commitment involved in the love of learning, tempered by a recognition of the dark forces in human nature that must be yoked in its service. Today in England and Italy, as in America, I find his name a touchstone of purposeful thought.

This year, on home leave, I brought my adolescent sons, one Italian-born, the other born in Germany, to their "fatherland" for the first time, partly so that they would know what they might have to be fighting for in a few years in another Vietnam, or, more hopefully, working to achieve for others in another Geneva. We visited an electronic computer plant in Phoenix one day, and were in the midst of 12,000 head of cattle in Tucson the next. Everywhere I showed them beautiful campuses (the American substitute for the Agora, the Forum, and Mont St. Michel), at Berkeley, Albuquerque, etc. Finally, we got to Columbia, with its jammed-in jumble of ugly red-brick Victorian, lofty neo-Classical, and, now, latticed neo-Moslem.

"What a funny place for a university," commented the "Italian." "Right on top of a subway."

"Yes," said the "German." "And you can't even tell the students from the citizens."

I guess that sums it up.

The Columbia
I Remember

⤜⤛✛✛⤜⤛

by Alfred A. Knopf

I didn't enter college as a conventional student. I wasn't graduated as one, and I haven't over the decades entertained the
affectionate feelings toward my alma mater that a college
has the right to expect of its alumni. Yet I have realized for
many years that Columbia bears a considerable responsibility
for whatever I have become—bad as well as good—and for
whatever I may have achieved or muffed the opportunity
of achieving. And I muffed plenty.

To begin with I haven't the faintest idea why I ever chose
to go to Columbia, for I knew nothing about the place at

ALFRED A. KNOPF, *1912 College, founded his own publishing firm three years later, and has richly colored the American
literary scene ever since. This essay is distilled from a talk
he made upon receipt of the 1966 Alexander Hamilton Award.*

first hand. There was no football team in those days, and the games I went to were always played at New Haven or Cambridge. Nor did Columbia particularly shine in track and field sports, which had my special interest. I was barely sixteen when I passed my college boards and thus became a freshman at much too young an age. Finally, I elected not to live on campus and, except for a few months one winter when the family took an apartment on West Seventy-seventh Street, I was a commuter. And the trip from Morningside Heights to Lawrence, Long Island, twice a day, took a lot of time.

However, my luck began almost immediately when James H. Canfield, then librarian of the University, became my faculty adviser. He was the father of Dorothy Canfield and had been chancellor of the University of Nebraska when Dorothy and Willa Cather were undergraduates there and very close friends. Undergraduates in 1908–09 had to take a half year both of physics and of chemistry. This was a tough requirement; for science was then, as it has ever since remained, a closed book to me; indeed it has simply passed me by, which makes it fortunate for me that I am not entering college today. Freshman physics in the fall of 1908 was a lecture course given by a distinguished man—(Ernest Fox) Nichols I think was his name—who couldn't have been less interested in freshmen. When the first examination came, I, with nearer a hundred than 90 percent of the class, failed. Worried, I went to Dr. Canfield and I have never forgotten what he said to me: "My boy, when I hire a shepherd to drive a flock of sheep from one town to another and he finds three who can set such a fast pace that the others never get there, I don't blame the sheep. I blame the shepherd."

Undergraduates in those days were free to roam all over the curriculum, and if you wanted to take courses for which you would get no credit toward a degree, that was your affair.

Sometime during freshman year I elected my first course in history. It was, I think, the second semester of History 1–2, the elementary course in General European History, which I had never studied at prep school. In one of the larger lecture rooms in Hamilton Hall, William R. Shepherd was holding forth on Philip II of Spain. I was entranced—absolutely spellbound. A new world was opened to me, and I suspect many of you know what history and historians have meant to me ever since. Will Shepherd remained a good friend to the time of his death. He was a fine man who, like many others, devoted himself to scholarship and students and published very little. As a matter of fact, he didn't write very well—it still amazes me how few historians do—and even in his letters there was a quaint, old-fashioned touch of stiffness. But he lectured superbly. It is a pity that he lived before a tape recorder could have saved for us the magnificent graduate course he gave on the expansion of Europe.

I must have enjoyed that freshman year, for I enrolled in summer school in 1909 and there attended what I suspect was the first course Carlton Hayes ever gave. He had just published his doctoral dissertation and was starting out on his great career. But even I could see that he was inexperienced, for he seemed to be very uncomfortable before the class and blushed all the time he spoke. We became good friends.

For the most part I took courses that I thought would interest me. Sometimes I guessed wrong, as in the case of anthropology with Livingston Farrand, later president of Cornell, and physiology with Russell Burton-Opitz, another poor fellow who could not have suffered undergraduates gladly. When examination time came he would sit in the back of the room muttering broad hints that suggested the correct answers to his questions.

I avoided Brander Matthews' very popular course on American Literature. I had a priggish notion, based on complete ignorance, that there was no such thing as American literature. But I did take courses in the drama with Brander, as everyone seemed to call him, and they were richly rewarding. In fact, I became so enamored of the theater that for a long time I went at least three nights a week, always sitting in the balcony where the best seats cost seventy-five cents.

Columbia's History Department during those years had many stars, and from them I drew one plum after another. The most celebrated course and perhaps the greatest was James Harvey Robinson's History 121–2 on the development of the intellectual class in Europe. Robinson was a small, soft-spoken, unexciting lecturer, but he really stretched your mind. I don't think anyone who took his course could ever have been quite the same again. Reading for it ranged from works in archeology and anthropology to the latest book by H. G. Wells.

After history came English and literature where my program was much less expansive. My favorite teachers were two very different types—John Erskine and Joel Spingarn. I recall especially a summer session course Erskine gave in composition because it was in it that I first became interested in language as a means of economical communication. The class had to write papers, now without using an adjective and again without using an adverb. Erskine was a very good teacher indeed, and we remained good friends for the rest of his days. I remember him drinking my father's brand of scotch at occasional lunches at the old Holland House on Fifth Avenue and sometimes at the Manhattan Club. Later, he blossomed out, the result I think partly of his experience in World War I, but chiefly of the enormous popular success of his first novel, *The Private Life of Helen of Troy*.

Joel Spingarn was a much more unconventional teacher but a really inspiring one. His enthusiasm for the classics, and indeed for good writing by anyone, was contagious. I was a member of the last undergraduate course he gave—Comparative Literature 1–2 in 1910–11. Although he was always able to hold our interest, he would frequently take a seat in the back of the room and ask one of the boys to conduct the class. All in all, his course seemed very easy indeed, and so we were outraged when at the end of the term we were handed a ridiculously difficult examination paper which none of us could possibly have passed. You can imagine our even greater astonishment to find, when the marks were posted on the bulletin board in Hamilton Hall, that every one of us had been given an A. Later we learned how this had come about. Spingarn was locked in battle, as other Columbia professors had been before him, with the administration, which was of course Nicholas Murray Butler. The issue revolved about a very popular and gifted but indiscreet member of the faculty, Harry Thurston Peck, reputed to have once advised his students, "Don't ever write. Telephone."

Somehow Peck was out of Columbia, fired as undergraduates believed, but more likely forced to resign. Spingarn protested so vigorously that he too soon resigned. We visited him at his home on West Seventy-third Street to express our feel-

ings of admiration and sympathy. There he told us that he
wanted to give us all something to remember him by, and
hence our A's. As he had already left the University, he had
to ask someone in the English Department to post the marks
for him. He wanted this done by the colleague who would
be most outraged by his grading, and seized on George C. D.
Odell, a stately, white-haired gentleman whose chief interest
was the history of the New York stage, which he recorded in
many volumes. Spingarn had gone right to the mark—Odell
was outraged and told me he felt that what Spingarn had
done was the most outrageously immoral act he had ever seen
committed during all his years at Columbia.

Spingarn's great influence on my life was outside the classroom and quite accidental as far as he was concerned. Every
year he gave three undergraduate prizes, one for a short story,
one for an essay, and one for a poem. I used to frequent Cox's
secondhand bookshop on 125th Street—there were a lot of
them there—and one day I bought a novel by John Galsworthy. The name was unfamiliar, and when I asked John
Erskine about Galsworthy he told me simply that he was an
Englishman who wrote plays for Charles Frohman. This reply didn't really do Galsworthy justice, for by 1911 he had
published many far from undistinguished novels, all of which
I read with immense pleasure. I decided to write an essay on
his work and enter it in the Spingarn contest. I wanted some
facts about Galsworthy's life and, being a very brash young
man, I addressed my inquiries to him. Rather to my surprise
he replied at length, and thus began a correspondence that
continued for the rest of his life and resulted in a close and in-
fluential friendship. I must add that my essay did not win the
prize, but I doubt whether, had I not met Galsworthy in

England in the summer of 1912, I would have become a publisher. I was to go to the Harvard Law School, and I recall with wry amusement that all I needed to be admitted there was to present my Columbia diploma.

Learning to Live

❧✦❧

by *Thomas Merton*

Life consists in learning to live on one's own, spontaneous, free-wheeling: to do this one must recognize what is one's own —be familiar and at home with oneself! This means basically learning who one is, and learning what one has to offer to the contemporary world, and then learning how to make that offering valid.

The purpose of education is to show a person how to define himself authentically and spontaneously in relation to his world. Not to impose a prefabricated definition of the world, still less an arbitrary definition of the individual himself. The world is made up of the people who are fully alive in it:

THOMAS MERTON (*the Reverend M. Louis, O.C.S.D.*), *1938 College, 1939 M.A., taught English briefly, became a Trappist monk, priest, and a writer of world renown.*

that is, of the people who can be themselves in it and can enter into a living and fruitful relationship with each other in it. The world is therefore more real in proportion as the people in it are able to be more fully and more humanly alive: that is to say better able to make a lucid and conscious use of their freedom. Basically, this freedom must consist first of all in the capacity to choose their own lives, to find themselves on the deepest possible level. A superficial freedom to wander aimlessly here or there, to taste this or that, to make a choice of distractions (in Pascal's sense) is simply a sham. It claims to be a freedom of "choice" when it has evaded the basic task of discovering who it is that chooses. It is not free because it is unwilling to face the risk of self-discovery.

The function of a university is then first of all to help the student to discover himself; to recognize himself, and to identify who it is that chooses.

This description will be recognized at once as unconventional and, in fact, monastic. To put it in even more outrageous terms, the function of the university is to help men save their souls, and in so doing to save their society: from what? From the hell of meaninglessness, of obsession, of complex artifice, of systematic lying, of criminal evasions and neglects, of self-destructive futilities.

It will be evident from my context that the business of saving one's soul means more than taking an imaginary object—"a soul"—and entrusting it to some institutional bank for deposit until it is recovered with interest in heaven.

Speaking as a Christian existentialist I mean by "soul" not simply the Aristotelian essential form but the mature personal identity, the creative fruit of an authentic and lucid search, the ultimate "self" that is found after other partial and exterior selves have been discarded as masks.

This metaphor must not mislead: this inner identity is not "found" as an object, but is the very self that finds. It is lost when it forgets to find, when it does not know how to seek, or when it seeks itself as an object. (Such a search is futile and self-contradictory.) Hence the paradox that it finds best when it stops seeking: and the graduate level of learning begins when one learns to sit still and be what one has become, which is what one does not know and does not need to know. In the language of Sufism, the end of the ascetic life is *Rida*, satisfaction. Debts are paid (and they were largely imaginary). One no longer seeks something else. One no longer seeks to be told by another who one is. One no longer demands reassurance. But there is the whole infinite depth of *what is* remaining to be revealed. It is not revealed to those who seek it from others.

Education in this sense means more than learning; and for such education one is awarded no degree. One graduates by rising from the dead. Learning to be oneself means therefore learning to die in order to live. It means discovering in the ground of one's being a "self" which is ultimate and indestructible, which not only survives the destruction of all other more superficial selves, but finds its identity affirmed and clarified by their destruction.

The inmost self is naked. Nakedness is not socially acceptable except in certain crude forms which can be commercialized without any effort of imagination. (Topless waitresses.) Curiously, this cult of bodily nakedness is a veil and a distraction, a communion in futility, where all identities get lost in their nerve endings. Everybody claims to like it. Yet no one is really happy with it. It makes money.

Spiritual nakedness on the other hand is far too stark to be useful. It strips life down to the root where life and death are equal, and this is what nobody likes to look at. But it is where freedom really begins: the freedom that cannot be guaranteed by the death of somebody else. The point where you become free not to kill, not to exploit, not to destroy, not to compete because you are no longer afraid of death or the devil or poverty or failure. If you discover this nakedness, you'd better keep it private. People don't like it. But can you keep it private? Once you are exposed . . . society continues to do you the service of keeping you in disguises, not for your comfort but its own. It is quite willing to strip you of this or that outer skin (a stripping which is a normal ritual and which everybody enjoys). The final metaphysical stripping goes too far, unless you happen to be in Auschwitz.

If I say this description is "monastic," I do not necessarily mean "theological." The terms in which it has been stated here are open to interpretation on several levels: theologically, ascetically, liturgically, psychologically. Let's assume that this last is the more acceptable level for most readers of these pages. And let's assume that I am simply speaking from experience as one who, from a French *lycée* and an English public school, has traveled through various places of "learning" and has, in these, learned one thing above all: to keep on going. I have described the itinerary elsewhere, but perhaps a few new ideas may be added here. The journey went from Europe to America, from Cambridge to Columbia. At Columbia, having got the necessary degrees, I crossed the boundary that separates those who learn as students from those who learn as teachers. Then I went to teach English at a Catholic College (St. Bonaventure). After which I went to be a novice in a Trappist monastery, where I also "learned" just enough theology to renounce all desire to be a theologian. Here also (for I am still in Kentucky) I learned by teaching: not theology as such, but the more hazardous and less charted business of monastic education, which deals with the whole man in a situation of considerable ambiguity and hazard: the novice, the young monk who wants to become a contemplative and who is (you sooner or later discover) trapped both by the institution and by his own character, into a situation where what he desperately wants beyond all else on earth will probably turn out to be impossible. Perhaps I would have been safer back at Columbia teaching elementary English composition. Fortunately I am no longer teaching anybody anything.

On the basis of this experience I can, anyhow, take up an ancient position that views monastery and university as having the same kind of function. After all, that is natural enough to one who could walk about Cambridge saying to himself "here were the Franciscans at one time, here the Dominicans, here—at my own college—Chaucer was perhaps a clerk."

A university, like a monastery (and here I have medievalists to back me up, but presume that footnotes are not needed), is at once a microcosm and a paradise. Both monastery and university came into being in a civilization open to the sacred, that is to say in a civilization which paid a great deal of attention to what it considered to be its own primordial roots in a mythical, archetypal holy ground, a spiritual creation. Thus the *Logos* or *Ratio* of both monastery and university are pretty much the same. Both are "schools" and they teach not so much by imparting information as by bringing the clerk (in the university) or the monk (in the monastery) to direct contact with "the beginning," the archetypal paradise world. This was often stated symbolically by treating the various disciplines of university and monastic life, respectively, as the "four rivers of paradise." At the same time, university and monastery tended to be in sometimes very heated conflict, for though they both aimed at "participation" in and "experience" of the hidden and sacred values implanted in the "ground" and the "beginning," they arrived there by different means: the university by *scientia,* intellectual knowledge, and the monastery by *sapientia,* or mystical contemplation. (Of course the monastery itself easily tended to concentrate on *scientia*—the science of the Scriptures—and in the university there could be mystics like Aquinas, Scotus, and Eckhart. So that in the end in spite of all the fulminations of the Cistercian St. Bernard, a deeper *sapientia* came sometimes from schools than from monasteries.)

The point I am making here is this. Far from suggesting that Columbia ought to return to the ideal of Chartres and concentrate on the *Trivium* and *Quadrivium,* I am insinuating that this archetypal approach, this "microcosm-paradise" type of sacred humanism, is basically personalistic.

I admit that all through the Middle Ages men were actively curious about the exact location of the earthly paradise. This curiosity was not absent from the mind of Columbus. The Pilgrim Fathers purified it a little, spiritualized it a little, but New England to them was a kind of paradise: and to make sure of a paradisic institution they created, of all things, Harvard. But the monks of the Middle Ages, and the clerks too, believed that the inner paradise was the ultimate ground of freedom in man's heart. To find it one had to travel, as

Augustine had said, not with steps but with yearnings. The journey was from man's "fallen" condition, in which he was not free not to be untrue to himself, to that original freedom in which, made in the image and likeness of God, he was no longer able to be untrue to himself. Hence he recovered that nakedness of Adam, which needed no fig leaves of law, of explanation, of justification, and no social garments of skins (Gregory of Nyssa). Paradise is simply the person, the self, but the radical self in its uninhibited freedom. The self no longer clothed with an ego.

One must not forget the dimension of relatedness to others. True freedom is openness, availability, the capacity for gift. But we must also remember that the difficult dialectic of fidelity to others in fidelity to oneself requires one to break through the veils of infidelity which, as individual egoists or as a selfish community, we set up to prevent ourselves from living in the truth.

This sacred humanism was of course abused and perverted by the sacred institution, and in the end monasticism, by a curious reversal that is so usual in the evolution of societies, identified the fig leaf with the paradise condition and insisted on the monk having at least enough of a self to serve the organization—itself pressed into the service of more mundane interests. Freedom then consisted in blind obedience, and contemplation consisted in renouncing nakedness in favor of elaborate and ritual vestments. The "person" was only what he was in the eyes of the institution because the institution was, for all intents and purposes, Paradise, the domain of God, and indeed God himself. To be in Paradise then consisted in being defined by the Paradisic community—or by Academe. Hence the dogmatic absolutism for which the late Middle Ages are all too well known—and for which they were by no means uniquely responsible.

The original and authentic "paradise" idea, both in the monastery (*paradisus claustralis*) and in the university, implied not simply a celestial store of theoretic ideas to which the *Magistri* and *Doctores* held the key, but the inner self of the student who, in discovering the ground of his own personality as it opened out into the ground of all created being, found in himself the light and the wisdom of his Creator, a light and wisdom in which everything comprehensible could be comprehended and what was not comprehensible could nevertheless be grasped in the darkness of contemplation by a direct and existential contact.

Thus the fruit of education, whether in the university (as for Eckhart) or in the monastery (as for Ruysbroeck), was the activation of that inmost center, that *scintilla animae,* that "apex" or "spark" which is a freedom beyond freedom, an identity beyond essence, a self beyond all ego, a being beyond the created realm, and a consciousness that transcends all division, all separation. To activate this spark is not to be, like Plotinus, "alone with the Alone," but to recognize the Alone which is by itself in everything because there is nothing that can be apart from It and yet nothing that can be with It, and nothing that can realize It. It can only realize itself. The "spark" which is my true self is the flash of the Absolute recognizing itself in me.

This realization at the apex is a coincidence of all opposites (as Nicholas of Cusa might say), a fusion of freedom and unfreedom, being and unbeing, life and death, self and nonself, man and God. The "spark" is not so much a stable entity which one finds, but an event, an explosion which happens as all opposites clash within oneself. Then it is seen that the ego is not. The ego vanishes in its non-seeing when the flash of the spark alone is. When all things are reduced to the spark, who sees it? Who knows it? If you say "God" you are destroyed, and if you say "no one" you plunge into hell, and if you say "I" you prove you are not even in the ball game.

The purpose of all learning is to dispose man for this kind of event.

The purpose of various disciplines is to provide ways or paths which lead to this capacity for ignition.

Obviously it would be a grave mistake to do, as some have done and still do, and declare that the only way is to be found in a cloister and the only discipline is asceticism or Zen sitting or, for that matter, turning on with a new drug. The whole of life is learning to ignite without dependence on any specific external means, whether cloistered, Zenist, Tantric, psychedelic, or what have you. It is learning that the spark, being a flash at the apex and explosion of all freedoms, can never be subject to control or to enticement, can never be got by pressing buttons. A spark that goes off when you swallow something or stick yourself with something may be a fairly passable imitation of the real thing, but is not the real thing. (I will not argue that it cannot teach you a great deal about the real thing.) In the same way a cloistered complacency, a "peace" that is guaranteed only by getting out of all the traffic and turning off the radio and forgetting the world, is not by itself the real thing either.

The danger of education, I have found, is that it so easily confuses means with ends. Worse than that, it quite easily forgets both and devotes itself merely to the mass production of uneducated graduates—people literally unfit for anything except to take part in an elaborate and completely artificial charade, which they and their contemporaries have conspired to call "life."

A few years ago a man who was compiling a book on success wrote and asked me to contribute a statement on how I got to be a success. I replied indignantly that I was not able to consider myself a success in any terms that had a meaning to me. I swore I had spent my life strenuously avoiding success. If it so happened that I had once written a best seller this was a pure accident, due to inattention and naïveté, and I would take very good care never to do the same again. If I had a message to my contemporaries, I said, it was surely this: be anything you like, be madmen, drunks, and bastards of every shape and form, but at all costs avoid one thing: success. I heard no more from him and I am not aware that my reply was published with the other testimonials.

Thus I have undercut all hope of claiming that Columbia made me a success. On the contrary, I believe I can thank Columbia, among so many other things, for having helped me learn the value of unsuccess. Columbia was for me a microcosm, a little world, where I exhausted myself in time. Had I waited until after graduation it would have been too late. During the few years in which I was there I managed to do so many wrong things that I was ready to blow my mind. But fortunately I learned, in so doing, that this was good. I might have ended up on Madison Avenue if I hadn't. Instead of preparing me for one of those splendid jobs, Columbia cured me forever of wanting one. Instead of adapting me to the world downtown, Columbia did me the favor of lobbing me half conscious into the Village, where I occasionally came to my senses and where I continued to learn. I think I have sufficiently explained, elsewhere, how much I owed, in this regard, to people like Mark Van Doren (who lived around the corner from me in the Village) and Joseph Wood Krutch (who became, as I have become, a hermit). Such people taught me to imitate not Rockefeller, but Thoreau. Of course I am not trying to say that one has to be Thoreau rather than Rockefeller, nor am I slyly intimating that I have discovered a superior form of resentment, an offbeat way of scoring on everybody by refusing to keep score.

What I am saying is this: the score is not what matters. Life does not have to be regarded as a game in which scores are kept and somebody wins. If you are too intent on winning, you will never enjoy playing. If you are too obsessed with success, you will forget to live. If you have learned only how to be a success, your life has probably been wasted. If a university concentrates on producing successful people, it is lamentably failing in its obligation to society and to the students themselves.

Many of my classmates at Columbia have attained to eminence with all its joys and all its sorrows and the ones I have seen since then are marked by the signature of anguish. So am I. I do not claim exemption. Yet I never had the feeling that our alma mater just wanted us to become well-paid operators, or to break our necks to keep on the front page of the *Times*. On the contrary—maybe this is a delusion, but if it is a delusion it is a salutary one—I always felt at Columbia that people around me, half amused and perhaps at times half incredulous, were happy to let me be myself. (I add that I seldom felt this way at Cambridge.) The thing I always liked best about Columbia was the sense that the University was,

on the whole, glad to turn me loose in its library, its classrooms, and among its distinguished faculty, and let me make
what I liked out of it all. I did. And I ended up by being
turned on like a pinball machine by Blake, Thomas Aquinas, Augustine, Eckhart, Coomaraswamy, Traherne, Hopkins,
Maritain, and the sacraments of the Catholic Church. After
which I came to the monastery in which (this is public knowledge) I have continued to be the same kind of maverick and
have in fact ended as a hermit who is also fully identified
with the peace movement, with Zen, with a group of Latin
American hippie poets, etc., etc.

The least of the work of learning is done in classrooms.
I can remember scores of incidents, remarks, happenings, en-
counters that took place all over the campus and sometimes
far from the campus: small bursts of light that pointed out
my way into the dark of my own identity. For instance Mark
Van Doren saying to me as we crossed Amsterdam Avenue,
"Well, if you have a vocation to the monastic life, it will not
be possible for you to decide not to enter" (or words to that
effect). I grasped at once the existential truth of this statement.

One other scene, much later on. A room in Butler Hall,
overlooking some campus buildings. Daisetz Suzuki, with his
great bushy eyebrows and the hearing aid that aids nothing.
Mihoko, his beautiful secretary, has to repeat everything. She
is making tea. Tea ceremony, but a most unconventional one,
for there are no rites and no rules. I drink my tea as reverently
and attentively as I can. She goes into the other room. Suzuki,
as if waiting for her to go, hastily picks up his cup and drains
it.

It was at once as if nothing at all had happened and as if
the roof had flown off the building. But in reality nothing

had happened. A very, very old deaf Zen man with bushy eyebrows had drunk a cup of tea, as though with the complete wakefulness of a child and as though at the same time declaring with utter finality, "This is not important!"

The function of a university is to teach a man how to drink tea, not because anything is important, but because it is usual to drink tea, or, for that matter, anything else under the sun. And whatever you do, every act however small, can teach you everything. Provided you see who it is that is acting.